THE CLASSIC
RAYBURN
BOOK OF
SLOW
COOKING

CW00422520

THE CLASSIC
RAYBURN
BOOK OF
SLOW
COOKING

Louise Walker

Absolute Press

First published in
Great Britain in 1998 by Absolute Press
Reprinted April 2000
Reprinted September 2003

Absolute Press
Scarborough House
29 James Street West
Bath BA1 2BT
England
Phone 44 (0) 1225 316013
Fax 44 (0) 1225 445836
E-mail info@absolutepress.demon.co.uk
Website www.absolutepress.demon.co.uk

© Louise Walker 1998

All rights reserved. No part of this
publication may be reproduced, stored
in a retrieval system or transmitted in
any form or by any means, electronic
or otherwise, without the prior
permission of Absolute Press.

A catalogue record of this book is
available from the British Library

ISBN 1 899791 17 5

Cover and text illustrations
by Caroline Nisbett

Printed and bound
by Lego Print Italy

Contents

INTRODUCTION

CONVERSION CHART

This is the metric/imperial chart that I abide by. Do keep to either metric or imperial measures throughout the whole recipe. Mixing the two can lead to all kinds of problems. Eggs used in testing have been size 3. Tablespoon and teaspoon measures have been flat unless otherwise stated.

1 oz	25g
2 oz	50g
3 oz	75g
4 oz	100g
5 oz	150g
6 oz	175g
7 oz	200g
8 oz	225g
9 oz	250g
10 oz	275g
11 oz	300g
12 oz	350g
13 oz	375g
14 oz	400g
15 oz	425g
16 oz (1 lb)	450g
2 lb	1kg
1 tsp	5ml
1 tbsp	15ml
¼ pint	150ml
½ pint	300ml
¾ pint	450ml
1 pint	600ml
2 pints	1.2l
8-inch tin	20-cm tin

AN INTRODUCTION TO SLOW COOKING

Everyone knows that Rayburns are brilliant for cooking food slowly. They are, of course, good for all other cooking methods, quick stir-fries, perfect pastry, moist cakes, let alone drying the washing and more besides.

But back to slow cooking. The gentle even heat of the oven set to simmer cooks food at an even temperature with little moisture loss, so casseroles, cakes and puddings will cook at an even pace and come out luscious and moist. Food cooking in the oven at this low simmering temperature will not dry out and spoil if it is not taken out at the precise time stated in the recipe, and, as all Rayburn-owners know, it is easy to leave food cooking longer than planned because no smells permeate the kitchen! I admit to having left stock and meringues in a low oven for at least three days! Although the food may be still edible and not totally spoilt after long cooking at the simmering temperature, the flavours will not be at their peak, meat will be too soft and vegetables may be mushy, so I have tried to give the optimum cooking time. All Rayburns are different: some models have a cast-iron bottom oven that will cook at half the temperature of the top oven, so food can be cooked slowly while the main cooking continues. Other Rayburns will have to have the main oven set to 'simmer' and the food cooked slowly there, sometimes even overnight. After a couple of test recipes do be prepared to adjust cooking times to suit your Rayburn. The settings given can only be approximate as all ovens vary. Most of these recipes will cook best at the higher end of the 'Simmer', unless you want to increase the cooking time. I have given a Centigrade and Gas Mark temperature chart as some Rayburns have these settings, however, with a Rayburn they can only be used as a guide.

There are a few rules to be followed when using the oven set on a low temperature. Apart from meringues, rich fruit cakes and porridge, food to be cooked at this lower temperature needs to be heated before it will cook at a lower temperature. Heat the food on the hot plate, making sure the food and the cooking pot are hot all the way through before transferring the oven; shelf positions don't matter at this lower temperature – it all depends upon what else you will be cooking at the same time. Cover food with a lid or foil to prevent drying out on the surface and a crust forming. Remember that filling the oven will lower the temperature, so allow extra time if you plan to cook for a large crowd.

A word about re-heating: casseroles, curries, etc., often have a better flavour if cooked a day in advance and then re-heated. All hot food should be served piping hot, so re-heat either in a hot oven or on the hot plate until not just bubbling but really hot. At this stage the dish can be held in a low oven or plate-warming oven.

I hope this book gives you some fresh ideas for dishes that can be popped in the oven at the beginning of the day and left to cook slowly without you standing over them; and to serve with the minimum of fuss at the last minute.

OVEN SETTINGS

Oven Setting	°C	Gas Mark
Simmer	140-160	1-3
Bake	180-210	4-6
Roast	220-260	7-9

GENERAL INTRODUCTION

I know from the demonstrating and workshop sessions I run, that there are two types of Rayburn owner: those who choose a Rayburn to put into their home and those who inherit a Rayburn when they move house. The former have either been brought up with a Rayburn, or they have had the opportunity to observe the multitude of benefits bestowed by the presence of a Rayburn. The latter are often terrified by the monster in the kitchen, but after only a few months, the fear has gone and they are quite converted.

We all love the constant warmth when the Rayburn is on. thus creating that heart to the kitchen. I have yet to find a Rayburn owner, new or old, who would change to another cooker, let alone give up all those other conveniences the Rayburn provides. The most popular selling Rayburns at the moment are gas-fired. However, not so long ago solid fuel was the popular fuel for Rayburns and some people still think that Rayburns can only be properly run on this. In fact many other fuels can be used: electricity, liquid propane, gas and oil.

The solid fuel Rayburns are the most complicated to run and, if yours is one of those, your own experience will tell you how to fuel it for the particular cooking task in hand. Fortunately this experience does not take long to acquire. As with all Rayburns, keep the lids down as much as possible; some people open the vent door to give an extra boost of heat during cooking. Rayburns converted from solid fuel to oil or gas often have personality differences. For example, the ovens may prove difficult to regulate for various recipes. However, personality differences are fairly typical of all Rayburns, as they are made individually and are sited and fuelled differently.

Like all new kitchen appliances, it takes time to get to know your Rayburn; perhaps this is the secret of the great Rayburn-owners' loyalty – it becomes a personality in the kitchen. However, all this means that writing recipes for a Rayburn can in no way be regarded as an exact science – so treat these as guidelines. I hope that they will give you ideas on the efficient use of your Rayburn and on its range of capabilities. You can then go on to experiment confidently with other recipes.

LOOKING AFTER YOUR RAYBURN

If you are doing a lot of cooking or entertaining, for example, at Christmas, turn up the Rayburn a little more than usual. If you are used to the chore of cleaning a gas or electric cooker, you will love the simplicity of keeping the Rayburn clean. Mine gets a thorough clean just once a year, when it is switched off for servicing; mine is gas-fired, an oil-fired one needs 6-monthly servicing. The night before servicing I switch off the Rayburn completely. After the breakfast is cleared away I set to on the cleaning and try to do as much as possible before the engineer arrives. Remove everything possible; the oven shelves and the doors which simply lift off. Brush out all the carbon deposits from the ovens. Anything still sticky on the floor of the oven can be removed with a wooden spatula, and the remains left to carbonise.

Clean the lids of the boiling plate, simmering plate and round the inside of the oven door frames with a warm soapy cloth and a paste cleaner such as Astonish. Never be tempted to use a wire wool pad or a tough abrasive. Some elbow grease may be needed but you will be surprised how much dirt will come off. Rinse off with a clean cloth and buff up. Clean the oven shelves in a sink of soapy water and more Astonish if needed. Wipe round the doors and clean the inside of the top and lower oven doors if necessary. The other doors will probably not get dirty. If you are concerned about the state of the seals remember to get the engineer to check them. Return all the bits and pieces to their places and give the whole Rayburn a wipe down and buff up. I know some people who polish their Rayburns occasionally! Other than the annual clean; try to wipe up any spills as they occur and wipe off any other crumbs, dust and so on daily. I find a lot of dust on my Rayburn, partly due to all the laundry put to dry or air above it.

POTS, PANS AND ACCESSORIES

Many people worry about their saucepans when they have a new Rayburn. If they are looked after, new pans purchased with a Rayburn will last a lifetime because there is no warping of the bases due to the even heat area. However, it isn't always necessary to rush out and buy pans. Think carefully about what you need and buy one at a time.

If you have existing pans there are two ways of testing their suitability for the Rayburn. Turn the pan upside down and put a ruler or something with a straight edge across the base. If daylight shows through; the pan will not work efficiently. Alternatively half-fill the pan with water and put on the boiling plate to boil. If only a poor contact is being made the water will not boil. Beware – even toast crumbs on the plate can have the same effect. A good, heavy-based pan is best. The size, shape and metal varies so choose according to your personal needs and preferences. Pans that go on the hot plates and in the oven are very useful. The Rayburn showroom will have a good range to show you.

A kettle is useful, but the shape and style is your own personal preference. Choose a heavy base and ask if you can do a water pouring test in the showroom or shop so that you know that the kettle suits you.

The Rayburn tin is useful because it fits the runners of the oven and can be used as a shelf. The roasting rack for the tin is handy to use when roasting fatty meat, or for grilling bacon, sausages and chops.

You will use ovenproof dishes quite a lot because so much cooking is done in the ovens. I find pans and casseroles that can be used on the top plates and in the oven especially useful but beware, wooden or plastic handles as those on the Rayburnluxe range cannot be used in the roasting oven. In time wooden handles will dry out and come apart. Cast-iron pans and dishes are useful for their multi-purpose use but they can be heavy to lift!

COOKING WITH THE RAYBURN

The Rayburn uses stored heat, and the ovens cook really well when they are evenly heated, so the aim is to cook with as little heat loss as possible. As soon as the hot plate lids are raised, heat will be lost, so use the ovens as much as possible. Of course, that way all the smells and condensation go up the chimney.

To maintain heat, the heavy insulated lids are kept down when the hot plate is not in use. The shiny lids are slightly domed. Do not be tempted to put the kettle or other pots and pans on the lid without using a protective pad – once scratched always scratched. Always remember – as soon as cooking is finished put the lids down so that heat is restored.

Frying, steaming and grilling can be done in the oven, while toast is done on the hot plate.

The ovens, which look so small from the outside, are very spacious inside. Rayburn roasting tins are designed to fit exactly so they will slide on the runners without the use of the oven shelf. Rayburns are now supplied with a roasting tin with rack to fit. The rack makes a useful cooling rack when you are doing a lot of baking. Two oven shelves with useful anti-tilt devices are also supplied. If you have the opportunity, try sliding the shelves in and out of the oven before the Rayburn is fired up. They are easy to use once you have the knack, but difficult to manage when hot if you have not tried it before. I know one couple who spent a whole day trying to get their shelves out!

The mysterious cold plain shelf is also supplied. This also fits the runners and can be used as an oven shelf or a baking tray. However, it should be kept out of the oven, somewhere cool, so that it can be used to diffuse the heat when the hot oven is used to cook foods at a lower temperature. I met one lady, a Rayburn owner for 30 years, who did not know what the cold plain shelf was really for. No wonder she thought my demonstration was a revelation!

TIPS AND USES
FOR THE RAYBURN

One of the best tips I can give when buying a Rayburn is to buy a timer you can carry around with you! There are no smells from the Rayburn oven, so it is easy to forget about food cooking inside. I think all Rayburn owners have opened the oven and thought "what was that lump of charcoal?" Those yellow sticky note pads are useful – reminders on the breakfast table to "remember porridge" or "remember stock/Christmas cakes/puddings, etc.". I have been known to put a reminder "remember casserole" on my pillow so that I remove it before going to bed.

Dry baking tins and awkwardly shaped cooking utensils on top of the Rayburn – there are no excuses for rusty tins.

Pastry cases for quiches do not need to be baked blind. Simply cook them directly on the floor of the roasting oven for a crisp base. It is safe to use porcelain, glass and metal flan dishes.

Stand mugs of tea or coffee on top of the Rayburn to keep warm when the telephone rings.

To defrost cakes or bread, stand them on top of the simmering plate lid or place in a simmering oven.

Dry the washing on top of the simmering plate lid – the boiling end is too hot. Spin the items to be dried, smooth out any creases and lay on the lid – no ironing needed! Hang towels or sheets over the chrome rail – just take care not to cover the air vents on the control box door.

If your kitchen ceiling is high enough, a kitchen maid above the Rayburn is useful for drying washing. Hang dried flowers on the ends so that it does not look too utilitarian.

Rugby boots washed of all their mud, and washed trainers, can be hung by their laces on the chrome rail and dried.

Shoes wet from winter rain should be stuffed full with newspaper and dried in front of the Rayburn – the gentle heat will not spoil the leather.

When the snow comes the Rayburn heat is busy not just producing hot food but drying snowy gloves and socks, as well as warming coats, hats and boots.

Finally, a word about oven gloves. Go for the long Rayburn gauntlets: no more burnt arms reaching to the back of the oven to get that elusive dish or potato.

BASIC RAYBURN TECHNIQUES

FISH

Although there are no recipes in this book for slow-cooked fish, I have included this basic guide as cooking fish in the Rayburn is so easy and cuts out fishy smells! The variety of fish available is increasing all the time, so experiment with different fish and different cooking methods. I have given approximate cooking times, but this will depend upon the size and thickness of the fish. Try not to overcook as this gives dry, stringy, tasteless fish.

POACHING FISH

Place the fish in the roasting tin, cover with water, wine or milk, add salt, pepper and a bayleaf. Hang the tin on the third set of runners from the top of the roasting oven for 15-20 minutes.

POACHING WHOLE LARGE FISH

Clean the fish. Sprinkle with salt if desired, and wrap in buttered foil, sealing well. Lift the parcel into the roasting tin, pour boiling water into the tin to come half-way up the fish. Hang on the second set of runners from the top of the roasting oven. Cook for 10 minutes per lb (450g), turning the fish half-way through cooking. Remove from the oven and allow to cool. Serve warm or remove the skin when cold.

FRIED FISH

Wash and dry the fish. If required, coat it with seasoned flour, batter, oatmeal or egg and fresh breadcrumbs. Put enough cooking oil into the roasting tin to coat the base. Put the tin on the floor of the 'roasting' oven and heat until hazing. Add the fish and continue to cook on the floor of the oven. Turn the fish half-way through the cooking time.

GRILLED FISH

Lay fish cutlets in a roasting tin, brush with oil and seasoning. Hang the tin on the highest set of runners and grill, turning half-way through the cooking time. It sometimes rings the changes to marinade the fish for half an hour and grill with the grill rack in the roasting tin, basting or brushing with a little more marinade part-way through cooking. This will give a more charred appearance and taste.

ROASTING MEAT

Meat roasted in the Rayburn will be moist and flavoursome. Only a smearing of extra fat is needed to start the cooking. Season as you prefer – salt, pepper, fresh herbs etc. If the meat is stuffed do this and then weigh to calculate cooking times. There are two methods of roasting using the Rayburn. The Quick Roasting Method is the more traditional method, used for more tender cuts of meat. The Slow Roasting Method is best for less fine cuts of meat.

QUICK ROASTING METHOD

Season the meat and put in the Rayburn roasting tin. Stand on the grill rack if you like. Hang the tin on the middle set of runners of the 'roasting' oven for the calculated time. Baste with hot fat periodically. The shape of the joint will also affect the cooking time – a long narrow joint will not take so long as a short, fat joint. When the meat is cooked, allow the joint to rest in the 'simmering' oven for 15 minutes before carving. This is useful time to make gravy and cook last minute green vegetables.

SLOW ROASTING METHOD

Season and prepare the meat as above. Put the roasting tin into the 'roasting' oven on the middle set of runners for 30 minutes or until the meat is browning and getting hot. Then transfer to the 'simmering' oven, and cook for twice the time calculated for the normal roasting method.

TIMES FOR ROASTING

ROAST BEEF

RARE	10 minutes per lb/450g, plus 10 minutes
MEDIUM	15 minutes per lb/450g, plus 15 minutes
WELL DONE	20 minutes per lb/450g, plus 20 minutes
FILLET	10 minutes per lb/450g, plus 10 minutes

ROAST PORK
30 minutes per lb/450g plus 30 minutes

LAMB

PINK	15 minutes per lb/450g, plus 15 minutes
MEDIUM	20 minutes per lb/450g, plus 20 minutes

VEAL
20 minutes per lb/450g plus 20 minutes

ROASTING POULTRY AND GAME

Roast poultry and game from the Rayburn will produce crisp skin on the outside of moist tender flesh. A lot of Rayburn owners like to cook their large turkey overnight in the 'simmering' oven. It is advisable to start the turkey in the hot 'roasting' oven for at least 45 minutes before moving to the simmering oven or turning the oven down to 'simmer'. This ensures the meat is hot. Finish the cooking by moving the bird to the 'roasting' oven for the final half-hour or raising the oven heat.

Smear the bird with a little butter. Put bacon rashers over the breast if liked. Stand on the rack in the roasting tin. Put lemon or herbs in the body cavity if liked. Hang the tin on the middle set of runners for the following times.

ROASTING TIME (IN THE ROASTING OVEN)

BIRD	WEIGHT	APPROX. COOKING TIME
CHICKEN	2lb / 900g	45–50 minutes
	3lb/1.5kg	1 hour
	4lb/1.75kg	1½ hour
	5lb/2.25kg	1¾ hours
TURKEY	8-10lb/3.5–4.5kg	1¾–2 hours
	11-15lb/5–7.25kg	2½ hours
	16-22lb/7.5–10kg	3 hours
DUCK		1–1½ hours
GOOSE		1½–2 hours
GROUSE		30–35 minutes
PIGEON		20–35 minutes
PARTRIDGE		30–35 minutes
PHEASANT		45–50 minutes
QUAIL		15 minutes
SNIPE		15 minutes
WOODCOCK		15 minutes

To test if cooked: pierce the thickest part of the thigh with a fine skewer, if the juices run clear the bird is cooked. Allow the bird to rest in the simmering oven whilst making gravy from the skimmed cooking juices.

BOILED BACON AND GAMMON JOINTS

Cooking a whole piece of ham in the Rayburn is so easy and gives a moist joint, perfect for slicing. I even cook ham for friends because they love the moistness and really it takes very little effort.

Soak the joint in water for 2–3 hours to remove any saltiness. Put a trivet or an old saucer in the bottom of a suitably sized pan. Put the joint on top and pour in enough cold water to come 2–3 inches up the side of the pan. Cover. Stand on the simmering plate and bring slowly to the boil and simmer for 30 minutes. Transfer the joint to the 'simmering oven' for the following times:

2–3 lb/900g–1.5kg	2½ hours
4–5 lb/1.75–2.25kg	3 hours
6–7 lb/2.75–3 kg	3½ hours
8–9 lb/3.5–4 kg	4½ hours
10–11 lb/4.5–5kg	5½ hours
12–13 lb/5.5–6kg	6½ hours
14–15 lb/6.5–6.75kg	7½ hours
16 lb/7.25 kg and over	overnight

Remove the pan from the oven and lift out the joint. Cool a little to handle. Strip off the skin and score the fat. Mix together a glaze of mustard and honey and spread over the surface. Stud with cloves if liked. Stand in a roasting tin with the glazing uppermost. Hang the tin so that the meat is in the middle of the roasting oven and bake for 10–20 minutes, until a golden glaze has formed. Watch it closely, it may burn! Serve hot or cold.

THICKENINGS

There are a variety of ways of thickening soups, stews and casseroles. The thickness of the gravy is largely a matter of personal taste, but also bear in mind what is to accompany the dish.

As an emergency thickener when time is short, a few instant thickening granuals can save the day. Keep a tub handy in the cupboard.

Cornflour is an easy and much used way of thickening at the end of cooking. Remember to 'slake' the cornflour with some water to make a smooth paste before adding to the hot food. Adding a little of the hot gravy to the cornflour also helps the blending process. Boil the casserole either on the simmering plate or in the oven for a few minutes until thickened.

Arrowroot is used in the same way as cornflour, but it will give a clearer, less cloudy finish to the gravy.

Reducing through boiling and then stirring in a knob of butter gives a glossy gravy, but never so thick as a gravy thickened with cornflour. Always strain the gravy off from the meat and vegetables before boiling so that the other ingredients are not spoilt by boiling. Boil the gravy rapidly to reduce to the required consistency. Whisk in a knob of butter at the end and pour over the meat and vegetables.

Buerre manié is a traditional French way to thicken gravies that gives a thickened, glossy sauce. Work together 1 tablespoon butter and 1 dessertspoon flour to make a paste. Drop small pieces of this mixture into the gravy and stir well whilst allowing to bubble gently on the simmering plate.

BOILED POTATOES AND OTHER ROOT VEGETABLES

Potatoes, along with other root vegetables, are best cooked in a slow oven. This both conserves the stored heat in the Rayburn and prevents the kitchen filling with steam. You will need to use a pan that can be used on the hot plate and in the 'simmering' oven, so no wooden handles. Do not be tempted to transfer the potatoes to a cold serving dish part-way through cooking – the entire heat of the pan, water and vegetables is needed for successful cooking.

Wash and prepare the potatoes in the usual way. Cut them to an even size. Place in the pan, add salt to taste and add about 2.5cm (1 inch) water. Cover and bring to the boil on the plate, boil for 1–2 minutes, drain off the water and then transfer to the 'simmering' oven. It is difficult to give timings, as the cooking time will depend upon the type and size of potato.

Allow 30 minutes and then test. Small new potatoes and small pieces of root vegetable will take about 20 minutes. Drain the vegetables, toss in butter if liked, and serve or return to the pan and the oven to keep warm.

ROASTING VEGETABLES

Roast vegetables are always a great favourite. I know that it is fashionably healthy to eat baked potatoes instead of roast, and steamed instead of roast parsnips, but nothing beats roast vegetables with roast meat for a special treat.

Peel and cut the vegetables to an even size. Boil for 1 minute in salted water, then drain thoroughly. While the vegetables are draining and drying put some cooking oil, lard or dripping into the roasting tin. Slide onto the floor of the 'roasting oven'. When the fat is hot tip in the dry vegetables, toss them in the fat and return to the oven, hanging the tin on one of the runners. If you are also roasting meat it may be necessary to juggle the tins during cooking. Cooking near the top will give an evenly cooked, crispy vegetable. Putting on the floor of the oven will crisp the bottom of the vegetables well. Vegetables take about 1 hour to roast. If the vegetables are put around the meat they may take longer and are often not so crispy, but they do taste wonderful!

RICE

A lot of people seem to have trouble cooking rice. Cooked in the oven of the Rayburn, it is very simple and can be kept hot without spoiling if you want to cook the rice slightly in advance. This is the basic method for cooking rice. Adjust the quantities to suit your needs. Use a saucepan that is happy both on the hot plate and in the oven.

1 cup rice
1 1/2 cups water
good pinch salt

Wash the rice in a sieve with cold, running water. Put in the saucepan. Add salt and water. Put on the lid.

Bring to the boil on the boiling plate. When boiling, transfer to the 'simmering' oven. Cook for the appropriate time. The times I have given produce a cooked, non-soggy rice. If you like your rice a little more cooked, then leave it in the oven for a little longer.

Remove the pan from the oven and drain the rice through a sieve – some types of rice will have absorbed all the water. If liked, rinse with boiling water. Serve.

Alternatively if you want to keep the rice hot, return to the pan and stir in a small knob of butter. Cover and return to the bottom oven until needed.

COOKING TIMES

WHITE LONG-GRAIN RICE	12 minutes
BROWN LONG-GRAIN RICE	20 minutes
BASMATI RICE	10 minutes

PASTA

Pasta needs a fast boil when cooking to prevent it sticking together. Try to use a pan that is deeper than its width. Half-fill with water, add salt to taste, cover and bring to the boil on the boiling plate. Add the pasta, fresh or dried, cover and bring to the boil – watch, this will not take long! Remove the lid and start timing according to the packet instructions. Alternativley transfer to one of the ovens. When the pasta comes to the boil, start timing. When al dente, drain through a colander, return to the pan and toss in a little oil or butter to prevent sticking. Serve straight away with a chosen sauce.

DRIED BEANS AND PEAS

The range of dried beans available in the shops gives a whole host of flavours, colours and textures for cooking. The beans and other grains can be used for vegetarian cooking or to make meat dishes go further or just to add variety. Lentils do not need soaking before cooking, just washing and picking over. All the other pulses need to be washed, picked over and left to soak for 8–12 hours or overnight – so some forethought is necessary.

Measure out the pulses required, wash well and pick over to remove any grit. Place in a bowl and cover with cold water. Put aside to soak.

Drain the liquid from the beans. Place in a saucepan, cover with cold water and bring to the boil. Boil rapidly for 10 minutes – to prevent boiling over use a large pan and no lid at this stage. After 10 minutes of rapid boiling, cover and transfer to the simmering oven until tender, 1–3 hours. The length of time depends upon the type and age of the bean. Experience will be your best judge. When cooked, use as per recipe.

PORRIDGE

We love porridge in the winter and it is a great favourite with a variety of toppings. I have to say that lashings of soft brown sugar comes top of the list, though I like fruit or salt – my husband favours yoghurt. This is the easiest breakfast dish to prepare, though if you are an infrequent maker of porridge you may need to leave a reminder on the breakfast table that some is in the oven! I have given a recipe for four servings, but I do know some people who make individual portions in a small cereal bowl with a saucer on top as a lid.

1 cup rolled porridge oats
1 cup water
2 cups milk
pinch salt

Put all the ingredients into a small saucepan, cover, and put in the simmering oven overnight. Stir and serve with milk or cream and your favourite flavouring.

PRESERVES

Home-made jams and chutneys are easy to make, though a little time consuming. Quite a lot of the cooking can be done in the simmering oven. This removes the need to watch the preserving pan all the time and prevents burning on the bottom of the pan. Jams or chutneys make wonderful presents, particularly when presented with an attractive label or in a pretty jar.

I am giving an outline for basic methods of preservation. For more detail HMSO publish *Home Preservation of Fruit and Vegetables* which is a really good reference book. Alternatively, my few recipes will give you the basic method and other recipes can be used. A good, large preserving pan will be needed. I use a large deep catering pan with a lid. With mine I can get the jam boiling well without too much spitting. The lid is useful when cooking slowly in the low oven. Collect jam jars with good, clean lids. I put mine through the dishwasher and keep them ready with their lids on. They only need warming in a lower oven when needed. Labels and wax discs are needed.

When making jam or marmalade here are a few basic tips: some fruit that needs slightly longer cooking, for instance, apricots, can be cooked in a 'simmering' oven until softened. Choose granulated or preserving sugar and always make sure it is dissolved before bringing to the boil, to prevent crystallising.

To test for set, remove the boiling jam from the heat after 10–15 minutes rapid boil. Put about 1 teaspoon of jam on a cold plate. Chill the sample for 1–2 minutes. If the surface wrinkles when pushed with the finger, the setting point has been reached. If the setting point has not been reached, boil again for 2–3 minutes and re-test. Too much boiling will give a syrupy jam. Cool the jam in the pan for a few minutes to prevent fruit rising to the top of the jar. Put the wax discs and lids on when the jam is either first put in the jar or when cold. Clean and label the jars when cold. Store in a cool, dark place.

SOUPS AND STARTERS

SOUPS AND STARTERS

Soups cook beautifully in a simmering oven. The basis of a good soup is a good stock which is made so easily in the Rayburn. This stock can of course be used for casseroles wherever stock is called for.

MEAT AND GAME STOCKS

Place the bones in a large saucepan with 2 or 3 flavouring vegetables, such as   onions, celery and carrots. Add some peppercorns and a bouquet garni. Just cover with cold water and bring to the boil on the hotplate. Skim any residue from the top. Simmer for about 10 minutes and then transfer to a simmering oven for 8–10 hours or overnight. Remove from the oven and strain through a sieve. Store the clear stock in the fridge or freeze in useful sizes.

VEGETABLE STOCK

Wash and chop a selection of vegetables. Place in a saucepan and add some peppercorns and a bouquet garni. Just cover with water and bring to the boil. Simmer for 10 minutes, then transfer to a simmering oven for 2–3 hours. Strain and discard the vegetables. Store in the fridge or freeze for later use.

Of course there are times when we all use stock cubes or powder. When seasoning the finished dish remember that these commercial stocks tend to be very salty, so season with care.

CREAM OF CHICKEN SOUP

....

This soup is a meal in itself. Any left-over chicken can be used for another dish, e.g. stuffed pancakes, pies, etc.

1 small chicken, about 1kg/2 lb 4 oz
1 large onion, chopped
2 celery stalks chopped
2 large carrots, sliced
1 leek, sliced
bouquet garni
blade of mace
rind and juice of 1 lemon
salt and pepper
40g/1½ oz butter
40g/1½ oz flour
2 egg yolks
150ml/¼ pint double cream

Put the chicken and vegetables into a large flameproof casserole. Add the bouquet garni, mace, lemon rind and juice, salt and pepper. Add enough water to just cover the chicken. Stand on the hotplate and bring to the boil. Skim off any scum and transfer to a simmering oven and cook for 1½–2 hours, or until the chicken is tender.

Remove the chicken and take the meat off the carcass. For the soup you will need 225–350g (8–12 oz) meat. Strain the stock and reserve about 1L/1¾ pints.

Melt the butter in a saucepan and stir in the flour. Whisk in the reserved stock, and bring to the boil and make a sauce. Add the chicken and heat through. Blend the egg yolk and cream and whisk into the sauce.

Serves 6

....

LEEK AND POTATO SOUP

This is possibly my favourite winter soup. It is easy to make and tastes delicious. The big green leeks I was once given in Wales made soup that I shall always remember – the flavour was outstanding!

50g/2 oz butter
1 onion, chopped
450g/1 lb leeks, trimmed, washed and sliced
2 potatoes, chopped
1L/2 pints vegetable or chicken stock
1 tsp salt
pepper
2–3 tbsp cream

Melt the butter in a large saucepan and sauté the onion and leeks until soft. Add the potatoes and toss in the butter. Cover and cook gently for a few minutes, until the potatoes are softening. Stir in the stock, salt and pepper. Cover and bring to the boil. Transfer to a simmering oven for an hour. Purée the soup, check the seasoning and serve in bowl with a little cream stirred in.

Serves 6

CELERY SOUP

....

This is a variation on the celery soup in The Classic Rayburn Cookery Book. The potatoes act as a thickening agent. Grated cheese at the end will make this into a substantial meal.

50g/2 oz butter
1 onion, chopped
1 head celery, washed and sliced
450g/1 lb potatoes, peeled and sliced
1 L/1³/₄ pints chicken or vegetable stock
salt and pepper
150ml/¹/₄ pint cream

Heat the butter in a flameproof casserole and sauté the onion, celery and potatoes. Cook gently until softening but not browning. Add the stock and a seasoning of salt and pepper. Cover, bring to the boil and transfer to a simmering oven for about 1 hour.

Purée the soup. Check the seasoning and pour in the cream just before serving.

Serves 4–6

....

FRENCH ONION SOUP

....

The long, slow cooking of the onions to caramelise them without burning is effortlesssly achieved in a simmering oven.

25g/1 oz butter
450g/1lb onions, sliced
1.2L/2 pints light stock
½ tsp salt
25g/1 oz flour mixed with 150ml/¼ pint water
4-6 slices French bread
50g/2 oz Gruyère cheese

Melt the butter in a large saucepan and stir in the onions. Cover and when the onions are piping hot, transfer to a simmering oven for an hour. Add the stock and salt, and bring back to the boil. Return to a simmering oven for a further hour. Stir in the flour mixture and boil for 2–3 minutes.

Place the French bread on a baking sheet, sprinkle on the grated Gruyère and toast for a few minutes at the top of the top oven. Place one piece in each soup dish and pour round the soup.

Serves 4–6

....

CRÉCY SOUP

....

This soup is named after the small town in France named Crécy that produces good root vegetables, especially carrots. 150ml/$\frac{1}{4}$ pint of orange juice can be stirred in at the end if you like carrot and orange soup.

75g/3 oz butter
225g/8 oz carrots, sliced
1 onion, sliced
salt and pepper
25g/1 oz white rice
1 sprig thyme
600ml/1 pint light stock

Melt the butter in a saucepan and sauté the carrots and onion. Season with salt and pepper, and cover. Allow the vegetables to sweat over a gentle heat for a few minutes. Add the rice, thyme and stock. Bring to the boil, transfer to the simmering oven for 1 hour. Remove the thyme and purée the soup. Check the seasoning and serve.

Serves 4

....

MINESTRONE

....

There are many variations on this recipe, largely depending upon the vegetables in season. Tiny pasta shapes can be added at the end of cooking, which particularly appeals to children.

100g/4 oz dried white cannellini beans or kidney beans,
soaked overnight
2 tbsp olive oil
1 large onion, finely chopped
2 carrots, finely diced
2 celery stalks, sliced
2 cloves garlic, crushed
2L/3½ pints chicken or vegetable stock
bouquet garni
½ small cabbage, finely shredded
2 courgettes, chopped
50g/2 oz mini pasta shapes
freshly grated Parmesan cheese, to serve

Rinse and drain the soaked beans. Heat the oil in a large flameproof casserole and sauté the onion, carrot, celery and garlic until softening but not colouring. Add the beans, the stock and bouquet garni. Cover and bring to the boil. Transfer to a simmering oven for 1½–2 hours.

Add the cabbage, courgettes and pasta shapes. Bring to the boil and return to a simmering oven for about 20 minutes. Check the seasoning. Serve with a little cheese on top.

Serves 8

....

LENTIL SOUP

....

This is a good soup to make if you have cooked a piece of ham, as the cooking liquid gives lentil soup a delicious flavour. Some crispy bacon can be served as a garnish if liked.

25g/1 oz butter
100g/4 oz lentils
2 carrots, diced
2 onions, chopped
1L/1³/₄ pints stock
salt and pepper

Heat the butter in a flameproof casserole and toss in the lentils. Add the carrots and onions, and sauté until the vegetables are softening.

Add the stock, bring to the boil, cover and transfer to a simmering oven for 1¹/₂–2 hours. Remove from the oven and purée the soup if liked. Check the seasoning and serve.

Serves 4–6

....

YELLOW SPLIT PEA SOUP

....

This is a substantial soup full of flavour from the ham. The peas used are not the green frozen variety!

275g/10 oz yellow split peas, soaked overnight
1 onion, finely sliced
2 celery stalks, chopped
piece of ham shank, soaked in water, about 450g/1 lb in
weight
sprig of thyme
salt and pepper
chopped parsley, to garnish

Rinse the split peas well and place in a large saucepan. Add the onion, celery, ham and thyme. Cover with 1.5L/2¾ water. Cover, bring to the boil and after 1–2 minutes transfer to a simmering oven for 2–3 hours, until the peas and ham are tender. Remove the ham and purée the split peas. Check the seasoning. Serve with pieces of ham in each bowl and garnish with chopped parsley.

Serves 4–6

....

ADUKI BEAN SOUP

Aduki beans are like small kidney beans. This recipe is adaptable to any dried pulses you may have in the store cupboard. Larger beans make take a little more time to cook.

2 tbsp vegetable oil
1 onion, chopped
1 celery stalk, chopped
1 carrot, diced
1 clove garlic, crushed
100g/4 oz aduki beans, soaked overnight
4 tomatoes, peeled and chopped
1 tbsp tomato purée
bouquet garni
1 L/1³/₄ pints water or light stock
salt and pepper
chopped parsley, to garnish

Heat the oil in a flameproof casserole and sauté the onion, celery, carrot and garlic until soft but not brown. Add the drained beans, tomatoes, tomato purée, bouquet garni and the water or stock. Cover and bring to the boil. Transfer to a simmering oven for 2 hours. Check the seasoning. Sprinkle with chopped parsley just before serving.

Serves 4–6

PÂTÉS

Pâtés are easy to make, especially with the aid of a food processor. However, if you like a coarse pâté, take care not to over-process the mixture. Alternatively, you can use a mincer. Pâtés can be cooked in a bain-marie in the oven set on 'Roast', alternatively cook for longer in the oven set on 'Simmer' after 30 minutes in the roasting oven. Always use the cold shelf if the oven is up to roasting temperature. If you think the pâté is crisping too much on the top, cover with a sheet of foil.

THRIFTY PÂTÉ

A good family pâté, economical and easy to make.

650g/1½ lb lean belly pork, roughly chopped
225g/8 oz pig's liver
100g/4 oz streaky bacon, rind removed
1 clove garlic, crushed
1 onion, chopped
1 tsp salt
pepper
¼ tsp ground coriander

Place all the ingredients in a food processor and process to make a smooth pâté. Press into a 1kg/2 lb 4 oz loaf tin. Stand in the roasting tin and pour boiling water round the loaf tin. Cover the loaf tin with a sheet of foil. Hang on the second set of runners from the bottom of the top oven set to 'Bake' or 150°C for 2 hours, slide the cold shelf on the runner above and cook for 30 minutes. Transfer to a simmering oven for 2-3 hours, until the pâté has shrunk from the sides of the tin. Weigh down the pâté and chill.

Makes 8–10 slices

FARMHOUSE PÂTÉ

....

A flavoursome pâté that should have a coarse texture.

100g/4 oz streaky bacon
225g/8 oz belly pork
225g/8 oz stewing veal
100g/4 oz pig's liver
salt and pepper
pinch powdered mace
2 tbsp white wine
1 tbsp brandy
2 cloves garlic, crushed

Remove the rind from the bacon. Reserve half the rashers and use these to line a 1kg/2 lb 4 oz loaf tin. Place the remaining ingredients in a processor and mince until all is chopped and blended, but not too fine. Press the mixture into the loaf tin. Stand the loaf tin in the roasting tin and pour round hot water to come about halfway up the sides of the loaf tin.

Slide on to the second set of runners from the bottom of the top oven set to 'Bake' or 150°C for 1½–2 hours, The pâté will have shrunk from the sides of the tin.

Chill the pâté and weigh down the top until completely cold.

Makes 8–10 slices

....

GAME PÂTÉ

A pâté to make in minutes using a food processor. This recipe uses only a small amount of game, but I find the meat from two pigeons gives an intensely flavoured, but not too rich pâté.

1 onion, chopped
25g/1 oz butter, melted
400g/14 oz sausage meat
½ tsp freshly grated nutmeg
2 tbsp brandy
salt and pepper
225g/8 oz game meat (e.g. pigeon)
1 egg

Put the onion, butter, sausage meat, nutmeg, brandy, salt and plenty of pepper into a food processor. Whizz round until all is mixed and the onion is chopped finely. Add the game and the egg, and whizz to just chop the meat and combine the egg.

Press into a 1.2L/2 pint oven-proof dish. Cover, and stand in the roasting tin. Pour boiling water round the dish. Hang on the second set of runners from the bottom of the top oven, set at 'Bake' or 150°C for 2 hours. Remove and chill before serving.

Serves 6

COARSE LIVER TERRINE

This is a coarse loaf rather than a smooth pâté. The sausage meat keeps the mixture moist and makes this an economical dish.

450g/1 lb pigs or lamb's liver
25g/1 oz butter
2 onions, chopped
100g/4 oz bacon, rind removed
100g/4 oz fresh breadcrumbs
225g/8 oz sausage meat
2 tsp Worcestershire sauce
1 tbsp lemon juice
salt and pepper
2 eggs, beaten

Remove any tubes from the liver and then roughly chop. Melt the butter in a frying pan and cook the liver and onions until golden brown.

Transfer the contents of the pan to a food processor along with the bacon, breadcrumbs, sausage meat, Worcestershire sauce and lemon juice. Whizz to just chop, then add salt and pepper, and the eggs. Whizz once more. Press the mixture into a 1kg/2 lb 4 oz loaf tin.

Stand the loaf tin in the roasting tin and pour water round to come about half-way up the sides of the loaf tin. Cover with a sheet of foil. Hang the tin on the second set of runners from the bottom of the top oven set 'Bake' 150°C for 2 Hours. The loaf can be served hot with a tomato sauce, or cold as a pâté.

Serves 8–10

HOUMMUS

....

This chick-pea spread can be eaten as a pâté. It is particularly nice with triangles of pitta bread and cold roast vegetables. My son Dominic likes it so much he has been known to eat it on hot-cross buns!

225g/8 oz chick-peas, soaked overnight
salt
4 tbsp tahini/(sesame paste)
2 cloves garlic, crushed
4 tbsp lemon juice, or to taste
2 tbsp olive oil

Drain the chick-peas and put in a saucepan, cover with water and bring to the boil on the hotplate. Cover and transfer to a simmering oven for 1½–2 hours, until the chick-peas are well cooked.

Drain the chick-peas, reserving some of the liquid. Transfer to a food processor with salt, the tahini, garlic, lemon juice and olive oil. Blend until smooth, adding some of the cooking liquid if necessary. Taste and add more lemon juice or salt as needed.

MAIN COURSES

PAPRIKA BEEF CASSEROLE

This recipe has a hint of Eastern Europe – the use of the paprika, combined with the tomato paste makes a thick, tasty sauce. If you don't have cider then use red wine instead for the marinade.

4 tsp paprika
6 tsp tomato purée
300ml/ 1/2 pint cider
1 tsp salt
1kg/2 lb 4oz stewing beef, cut into large dice
2 tbsp vegetable oil
2 onions, sliced
3 carrots, thickly sliced

Mix together the paprika, tomato purée, cider and salt in a non-metallic bowl. Stir in the beef, coat well and cover. Leave to marinate for about 8 hours or overnight.

Heat the oil in a flameproof casserole and sauté the onion and carrots until softening. Stir in the beef and the marinade. Bring to the boil. Add a little water if necessary. Cover and transfer to a simmering oven. Cook for 4–5 hours. The finished dish should produce its own thick gravy.

Serves 6

POT ROAST BEEF IN RED WINE

This is a delicious way to cook topside or silverside, which can be rather dry when plainly roasted. The vegetables give richness to the meat and make a wonderful sauce.

2 tbsp cooking oil
1kg/2.2 lb silverside or topside beef
2 carrots, cut into large dice
2 parsnips, cut into large dice
1 large onion, cut into quarters
2 cloves garlic, crushed
2 tbsp tomato purée
2 bay leaves
pinch sugar
salt and pepper
1/2 bottle red wine

Heat the oil in a flameproof casserole and brown the meat all over. Remove to a plate. Add the prepared vegetables to the casserole and sauté until just beginning to colour. Sir in the tomato purée, bay leaves, sugar, salt and pepper, and wine. Place the meat on top. Cover and slowly bring to the boil on the hotplate. Simmer for 10 minutes and then transfer to a simmering oven for 3–4 hours.

To serve: the braising vegetables may be served as they are or puréed to make a sauce. Slice the meat into thick slices.

Serves 6

DAUBE DE BOEUF

This must be one of the easiest casserole recipes. I have adapted this from my much-used *French Provincial Cooking* by Elizabeth David. A flameproof casserole dish with a tight fitting lid is best. This doesn't work so well in an electric oven, it is best simmering on a thread of heat on the hob, but of course it works brilliantly in a low simmering oven.

175g/6 oz unsmoked streaky bacon, rinded and cubed
2 tbsp olive oil
2 onions, sliced
2 carrots, sliced
2 tomatoes, peeled and sliced
1kg/2 lb 4oz braising or top rump beef
bouquet garni
2 cloves garlic, lightly crushed
salt and pepper
125ml/4 fl oz red wine

Lay the bacon in the base of the casserole dish, along with the olive oil. Then layer in the onions and carrots and the tomatoes. Lay on the meat and bury the bouquet garni and garlic amongst the meat. Season with salt and pepper. Stand on the cooler end of the hotplate and start warming through gently.

Pour the wine into a small saucepan and bring it to a fast boil. Set it alight. When the flames have died down pour the wine over the meat. Cover with a lid, make sure the casserole is thoroughly heated and then transfer to a simmering oven for 3-4 hours. This is often served with pasta that has been tossed with the fat from the top of the meat.

Serves 6

PROVENÇAL BEEF STEW

This is a simple beef casserole made a little different by the addition of black olives at the end of cooking. Olive oil used for the frying process will help give the Mediterranean flavour.

700g/1½ lb stewing beef
2 tbsp seasoned flour
4 tbsp olive oil
4 carrots, sliced
2 onions, chopped
2 cloves garlic, crushed
100g/4 oz mushrooms, sliced
300ml/½ pint red wine
150ml/¼ pint beef stock
about 12 black olives
salt and pepper

Cut the meat into large cubes and toss in the seasoned flour. Heat the oil in a frying pan and brown the meat. Transfer to a casserole dish. Cook the carrots, onions and garlic in the hot pan until the onions are softening and only slightly coloured.

Add the mushrooms, the red wine and stock, and bring to the boil. Pour over the meat. Cover, bring to the boil and transfer to a simmering oven for 3–4 hours. Add the olives and check the seasoning before serving.

Serves 6

CLASSIC BEEF CASSEROLE

A simple beef casserole using store-cupboard ingredients and a cheaper cut of meat. The flavour will be good after the long, slow cooking. For variety, the mustard may be replaced with 2 tablespoons of chutney.

700g /1½ lb beef skirt
25g/1 oz seasoned flour
1 tbsp vegetable oil
25g 1 oz butter
1 large onion, chopped
3 carrots, thickly sliced
2 tsp mustard
450ml/¾ pint beef stock

Cut the meat into large cubes and toss in the seasoned flour. Heat the oil and butter in a large frying pan and brown the meat on all sides. Drain and place in a casserole dish.

In the heated pan, sauté the onion and carrots until the onion is just starting to colour and slightly soften. Add to the meat. Stir the mustard into the pan and scrape off any residue from the base of the pan before stirring in the stock. Stir well, bring to the boil and pour over the meat. Bring to the boil and transfer to a simmering oven for 4–5 hours. Thicken the gravy (see page 21) if liked before serving.

Serves 6

MEXICAN CHILLI CON CARNE

This recipe originated in Mexico as a way of using up stringy beef. I cook it and serve it in taco shells or with rice for a crowd of people. Soured cream and guacamole are delicious spooned on top.

2 tbsp vegetable oil
2 large onions, finely chopped
350g/12 oz minced beef
350g/12 oz minced pork
2 cloves garlic, crushed
2 tsp chilli powder
1 tbsp dried oregano
1 tbsp cumin seeds, lightly crushed
450g/1 lb tomatoes, peeled and seeded
1 tbsp red wine vinegar
1 tsp sugar
salt and pepper
300g/11 oz cooked red kidney beans, or a large can, drained

Heat the oil in a large flameproof casserole and sauté the onion until soft. Add the meats and stir over a high heat until broken up and browned. Add the garlic, chilli powder, oregano, cumin seeds and tomatoes, stir well and bring to the boil. Add the wine vinegar, sugar, and salt and pepper. Cover and transfer to a simmering oven for at least 1 hour.

Remove from the oven and skim any fat and then stir in the kidney beans. Return to the oven for a further half 30 minutes. Adjust seasoning and serve.

Serves 6

STEAK AND KIDNEY PUDDING

An old British pudding traditionally served with a starched napkin tied over the top. The gentle cooking in the simmering oven lends itself to cooking this dish.

700g/1½ lb stewing beef, cubed
225g/8 oz ox or lamb kidney, cored and cubed
25g/1 oz seasoned flour
1 large onion, chopped
1 tbsp chopped parsley
salt and pepper
about 150ml/¼ pint beef stock

Suet Pastry
450g/1lb self-raising flour
225g/8 oz shredded suet
pinch of salt

To make the pastry, sift the flour, mix with the suet and salt, and enough water to bind. Toss the beef and kidneys in the seasoned flour. Line a 1.7L/3 pint pudding basin with three-quarters of the suet pastry. Fill the basin with alternate layers of steak, kidney and onions. Sprinkle each layer with parsley and a little salt and pepper. Add enough stock to just cover the meat. Use the remaining pastry to make a lid for the pudding. Seal the lid firmly. Cover with a layer of pleated greaseproof paper followed by foil or a pudding cloth.

Stand the basin in a saucepan deep enough to take the pudding with a lid on. Pour sufficient boiling water into the pan to come halfway up the sides of the basin. Cover and bring to the boil and simmer for 30 minutes on the hotplate before transfering to a simmering oven for 6 hours.

Serves 6

STEAK AND KIDNEY PIE

The pie can be topped with shortcrust or puff pastry, but the puff pastry looks most spectacular when served. There are many variations on this recipe – mushrooms can be added, Worcestershire sauce used for flavouring, plain stock and no tomato purée used. Some regions pour in cream just before serving!

675g/1 lb 8oz stewing steak, cubed
225g/8 oz kidneys, cored and chopped
1 tbsp seasoned flour
2 tbsp vegetable oil
1 large onion, chopped
300ml/½ pint beef stock
150ml/¼ pint red wine
1 tbsp tomato purée
1 tbsp chopped parsley
salt and pepper
225g/8 oz puff pastry
a little beaten egg, to glaze

Toss the steak and kidney in the seasoned flour. Heat the oil in a pan and brown the meat well. Transfer to a casserole dish. Add the onion to the hot fat and fry for a minute or two. Stir the stock, red wine, tomato purée, parsley, salt, pepper and onion into the meat. Bring to the boil, cover and transfer to a simmering oven for 4–5 hours.

Place the meat mixture in a pie dish and roll out the pastry to fit. Place a ceramic pie funnel in the middle of the pie dish and dampen the edges of the dish. Place a strip of pastry round the edge of the dish. Dampen then cover the pie with the pastry. Make a hole in the centre and decorate the edges. Brush with beaten egg. Place in the top oven set to roast, on the third set of runners from the top for 25–30 minutes until the pastry is puffy and golden brown.

Serves 6

CARBONNADE OF BEEF

A rich casserole of beef cooked slowly and topped off with slices of crisp mustard-coated French bread. Add the bread at the last moment otherwise the base of the bread will be soggy!

700g/1lb 8 oz braising steak, sliced
1 tbsp seasoned flour
1 tbsp vegetable oil
50g/2 oz butter
50g/2 oz streaky bacon, rinded and diced
3 large onions, sliced
300 ml/¹/₂ pint brown ale
150 ml/¹/₄ pint beef stock
5 tsp mustard
bouquet garni
salt and pepper
6 thick slices French bread

Toss the beef in the flour. Heat the oil and butter in a frying pan and brown the bacon. Transfer to a casserole dish.

Sauté the onions in the hot fat until softening but not browning. Drain and transfer to the casserole dish. Brown the meat on all sides and then add to the bacon and onions in the casserole. Sprinkle any remaining flour into the frying pan and stir well. Gradually whisk in the brown ale, the stock and one teaspoon of the mustard. Bring to the boil and pour over the meat in the casserole. Add the bouquet garni, cover and bring to the boil. Transfer to a simmering oven for 2–2¹/₂ hours.

Remove bouquet garni, and check the seasoning. Spread one side of each piece of bread with the remaining mustard and place on top of meat, mustard side uppermost. Place the casserole, without the lid, on the highest shelf that it will fit on in the top oven, raised to 'roast'. for 15–20 minutes, until the bread is crisp.

Serves 6

BRAISED OXTAIL CASSEROLE

This is a classic winter dish that has a full flavour. Cooking in a low oven brings out all the flavours. Oxtail can be a little fatty, so if this is made the day before serving, the fat can be skimmed off the top.

1 whole oxtail, cut into pieces
salt and pepper
2 tbsp vegetable oil
1 tbsp flour
25g/1 oz butter
1 large onion, finely chopped
2 large carrots, finely diced
4 celery stalks, finely sliced
300ml/1/2 pint red wine
1 tbsp tomato paste
1 bouquet garnis
600ml/1 pint beef stock

Season the oxtail with salt and pepper. Heat the oil in a frying pan and brown the oxtail pieces all over. Remove and place in a casserole dish. Sprinkle the flour over the oxtail pieces.

Wipe out the frying pan and melt the butter in it. Sauté the onion, carrots and celery until starting to soften. Pour on the wine, bubble for a minute and then stir in the tomato paste. Add the bouquet garni to the meat and pour on the wine and vegetable mixture. Add the stock, cover, bring to the boil and then place in a simmering oven for 4–5 hours, until the meat is tender and coming off the bone. The sauce may be skimmed and strained before serving.

Serves 4

PRESSED SALT BEEF

....

Salt beef can be bought from a traditional butcher. When cooked and pressed it slices thinly for sandwiches and salads. Keep it wrapped in greaseproof paper in the fridge.

2kg/4 lb 8 oz salted brisket of beef
1 onion, stuck with cloves
1 large carrot, thickly sliced
1 stick celery
1 bouquet garni
12 peppercorns

Soak the meat in cold water for 1 hour then drain. Place the meat in a saucepan or flameproof casserole along with the remaining ingredients. Just cover with fresh water. Bring to the boil, then transfer to a simmering oven for 4–5 hours.

Remove the meat, stand on a plate and press under a heavy weight for several hours until cold and set. Serve thinly sliced.

Serves 12

....

BRAISED AND SPICED TOPSIDE OF BEEF

Topside of beef can be a little on the dry side, so braising is a good, moist way to cook it. This is an easy way to cook a joint of beef for a large number of people. It is delicious served cold in thin slices. The cooking onions can be served with the hot meat or made into a tasty soup if the meat is served cold.

2kg/4 lb 8oz topside, boned and rolled
2 tsp salt
1 tsp ground allspice
3 tsp ground ginger
450ml/³⁄₄ pint cider
1 cinnamon stick
6 cloves
1 tbsp black peppercorns
2 blades mace
2 tbsp olive oil
2 onions, sliced
1 large carrot, sliced

Wipe the beef and rub with the salt, allspice and ginger. Put the cider, cinnamon stick, cloves, peppercorns and mace into a saucepan and bring to the boil. Put the meat in a non-metallic dish and pour over the cider mixture. Allow to cool and then marinade in a cool place for 48 hours, turning periodically. Heat the oil in a large frying pan. Pat the meat dry and brown all over in the hot pan. Transfer to a casserole dish, or the roasting tin. Add the vegetables to the hot pan and sauté until just softening. Add to the meat. Pour the marinade into the hot frying pan and bring to the boil. Pour over the meat.and simmer gently on the hotplate for 30 minutes, then transfer to the oven set to 'simmer' for 3–4 hours, depending upon the thickness of the beef joint and how rare you like the meat.

Serves 8-10

BOLOGNESE SAUCE

For a rich, fully-flavoured sauce cook this slowly in a simmering oven. This sauce freezes well, so I usually make a large quantity at a time and use to make lasagnes as well as spaghettis. This makes enough lasagne for 6.

2 tbsp olive oil
450g/1 lb lean minced beef
2–3 rashers bacon, rinded and chopped
1 onion, finely chopped
1 carrot, finely chopped
1 small celery stalk, finely diced
1 clove garlic, crushed
50g/2 oz mushrooms, finely diced
400g/14 oz can chopped tomatoes
1 tbsp tomato purée
1 bay leaf
150ml/1/4 pint red wine
pinch dried oregano
salt and pepper

Heat the oil in a flameproof casserole and fry the minced beef and bacon until browned. Drain and reserve. Sauté the onion, carrot and celery until softening. Add the garlic and the mushrooms, and cook for 1 or 2 more minutes.

Return the meat to the pan, add the tomatoes, tomato purée, bay leaf, red wine, oregano, and salt and pepper. Stir well, bring to the boil, cover and transfer to a simmering oven for 1–2 hours.

Serves 6

BEEF LASAGNE

....

A very popular dish – good when catering for a crowd, but can be time-consuming to make. Cook the sauce slowly for a good rich flavour.

2 tbsp olive oil
2 onions, finely chopped
2 cloves garlic, crushed
1kg/2 lb 4 oz good quality minced beef
225g/8 oz mushrooms, finely chopped
400g/14 oz can chopped tomatoes
3 tbsp tomato purée
150ml/1/4 pint red wine
1 tbsp chopped fresh basil, or 1/2 tsp dried oregano
2 bay leaves
salt and pepper
60ml/1 pint milk
50g/2 oz flour
50g/2 oz butter
225g/8 oz ready-to-use lasagne
75g/3 oz grated Gruyère cheese

In a flameproof casserole heat the olive oil and sauté the onion. When soft but not coloured, add the crushed garlic and the minced beef. Stir to break up the meat, and fry until brown. Add the mushrooms and fry for 2–3 minutes, then add the tomatoes, tomato purée, red wine, herbs, bay leaves, and a seasoning of salt and pepper. Cover, and bring to the boil, then transfer to a simmering oven for 1–2 hours. Butter an oblong oven-proof dish. Put the milk, flour, butter and salt and pepper into a saucepan and whisk over a medium heat until smooth. Spoon a little sauce into the base of the buttered dish. Lay on a layer of lasagne sheets and then a layer of meat sauce. Continue layering, finishing with lasagne and a topping of the sauce. Sprinkle on the grated cheese. Place the oven shelf on the bottom set of runners of the top oven set to 'Bake' and cook the lasagne for 40–50 minutes until golden brown, bubbling and the lasagne is cooked.

Serves 4-6

....

MAURITIAN CHICKEN CURRY

....

I made this recipe of Anton Mosimann's with squid for a cookery demonstration. Having some spices left I decided to use chicken for my family, and it works very well. It is not hot – add more chilli if you like it hot – but full of flavour.

1 tbsp coriander seeds
1 tsp cumin seeds
3 small shallots, chopped
2 cloves garlic
1 tsp finely chopped fresh ginger,
1 stalk lemon grass, chopped
3 fresh red chillies, seeded
2 tsp curry powder
1 tsp salt
2 tbsp vegetable oil
4 chicken portions, skinned
4 tomatoes, peeled, seeded and chopped
200ml/7 fl oz canned coconut milk
200ml/7 fl oz chicken stock
pepper

Dry-fry the coriander and cumin seeds in a frying pan. Place in a food processor or blender along with the shallots, garlic, ginger, lemon grass, chillies, curry powder and salt. Blend together to make a paste. Heat the vegetable oil in a flameproof casserole and brown the chicken. Remove and set aside. Sauté the curry paste in the hot casserole for about 5 minutes, stirring. Add the tomatoes, milk, stock and pepper, and bring to the boil.

Add the reserved chicken, cover and bring back to the boil, then cook in a simmering oven for 2–3 hours. Check the seasoning and serve.

Serves 4

....

HANNA'S CHICKEN WITH PEPPERS

This dish makes the most of those glorious looking red and green peppers. This is a great summer dish served with crisp salad and crusty bread. We have even eaten it cold as a salad, with the vegetables tossed in olive oil. The dish is named after my daughter who loves peppers and mushrooms.

1 tbsp olive oil
6 chicken portions
1 onion, sliced
1 clove garlic, crushed
1 large red pepper, seeded and cut into thick slices
1 large green pepper, seeded and cut into thick slices
175g/6 oz mushrooms, sliced
225g/8 oz tomatoes, skinned and sliced
150ml/1/4 pint white wine
1 tbsp tomato purée
salt and pepper
sprig fresh thyme

Heat the oil in a flameproof casserole and brown the chicken portions well. Drain and set aside.

Sauté the onion, garlic and peppers until softening, then add the mushrooms, tomatoes, wine, tomato purée, and salt and pepper. Add the thyme and push the chicken portions well into the vegetable mix. Cover and bring to the boil. Place in a simmering oven for 1 1/2–2 hours.

Serves 6

CHICKEN AND DRIED FRUIT TAJINE

A tajine is a deep earthenware pot from the Middle East that gives its name to a stew – in this case chicken and dried fruits. Couscous is a very good accompaniment.

1 large chicken, jointed, or 6 chicken portions
1 lemon, halved
salt and pepper
2 onions, finely chopped
1 clove garlic, finely chopped
$1/_2$ tsp ground cumin
$1/_2$ tsp powdered saffron or pinch saffron strands
2 tbsp olive oil
1 cinnamon stick
1 strip lemon peel
300ml/$1/_2$ pint chicken stock
225g/8 oz dried fruit, such as prunes, apricots and dates,
soaked, stoned and halved
3 tbsp clear honey
1 tbsp chopped fresh coriander
2 tbsp flaked almonds, sautéd in butter until pale gold

Rub the chicken all over with the lemon halves. Season with salt and pepper, and place in a dish. Mix together the onions, garlic, cumin, saffron and olive oil, and pour over the chicken. Mix well and leave to marinate, for at least an hour.

Skim the oil from the marinade into a frying pan and heat. Fry the chicken pieces, onion and garlic until golden brown. Drain and place in a casserole dish.

Add the cinnamon, lemon peel and stock to the casserole. Cover and bring to the boil, then place in a simmering oven for 1½ hours, until tender. Remove the chicken and place on a plate in a simmering oven to keep warm.

Add the dried fruits and honey to the casserole, bring to the boil, then transfer to the roasting oven for 15 minutes. Strain out the fruits and add to the chicken. Boil the remaining liquid over a high heat to reduce to a coating consistency. Return the chicken and fruit to the sauce to bubble through. Garnish with the coriander and almonds.

Serves 6

COQ AU VIN

....

Coq au Vin must be one of the most popular ways of cooking a chicken casserole. The combination of flavours works really well. The flavour of this dish really benefits from long, slow cooking.

2 tbsp olive oil
1 large chicken, jointed, or 6–8 chicken portions
1 onion, finely chopped
2 cloves garlic, crushed
100g/4 oz streaky bacon, rinded and chopped
150ml/1/4 pint chicken stock
12 shallots, peeled
450ml/3/4 pint red wine
salt and pepper
1 tsp dried tarragon
2 bay leaves
100g/4 oz button mushrooms
1 tbsp cornflour

Heat the oil in a large frying pan and brown the chicken joints. Drain and place in a large casserole dish. Add the onion and bacon to the pan and fry until the onion has softened, adding the garlic for the last minute. Drain and transfer to the casserole dish.

Add the wine to the pan and bring to the boil, then add the stock, salt and pepper, and tarragon. Bring to the boil and pour over the chicken.

Bury the shallot and bay leaves in the casserole. Cover and transfer to a simmering oven, for 1½ hours.

Stir in the mushrooms and return to the oven for a further 30 minutes. Blend the cornflour with water to make a smooth paste and stir into the casserole juices. Return to the oven for a further 15 minutes, until the sauce is thickened.

Serves 6–8

....

PEANUT CHICKEN CASSEROLE

The peanut butter makes a rich, moist sauce for the chicken and the whole peanuts add a delicious crunch.

6 chicken joints
2 tbsp seasoned flour
3 tbsp olive oil
1 onion, chopped
125ml/¼pint chicken stock
300ml/½ pint milk
2 tbsp smooth peanut butter
salt and pepper
3 tbsp single cream
50–75g/2–3 oz salted peanuts, roughly chopped

Coat the chicken portions with the seasoned flour. Heat the oil in a frying pan and cook the onion until soft. Drain and place in a casserole dish. Add the chicken to the hot oil and brown all over. Move to the casserole dish.

Add the stock to the pan along with the milk and peanut butter,bring to the boil, scraping all the residue from the base of the pan. Pour over the chicken. Season with salt and pepper. Cover the casserole and bring to the boil. Transfer to a simmering oven for 1–1½ hours. Stir in the cream and check the seasoning. Sprinkle over the peanuts.

Serves 6

CHICKEN IN A POT

Choose a casserole dish that is large enough to hold your chicken whole with some room for the vegetables. If you want to use a larger chicken, increase the amount of vegetables to go with it.

1.5kg/3 lb chicken
1 tbsp vegetable oil
4 celery stalks, cut into thirds
1 leek, cut into thick rings
4 carrots, peeled and thickly sliced
2 onions, peeled and quartered
100g/4 oz button mushrooms
1 bouquet garni
300ml/1/2 pint chicken stock
salt and pepper

Heat the oil in a frying pan and brown the chicken all over – especially the breasts. Transfer to a plate.

Sauté the celery, leek, carrots and onion in the hot fat for 2–3 minutes, then add the mushrooms. When the vegetables are starting to soften, transfer them to a casserole dish. Add the bouquet garni and place the chicken on top. Pour over the stock and season with salt and pepper. Bring the casserole to a gentle boil and then transfer to a simmering oven for 4 hours. The chicken should be cooked but the vegetables should still have some 'bite' left.

Serves 4

CHICKEN IN SHERRY SAUCE

A variation on chicken in wine! This is very simple to make and a useful way to use up the end of a bottle of sherry!

4 chicken portions
rind and juice of 1 lemon
150ml/1/4 pint sweet sherry
150ml/1/4 pint light chicken stock
50g/2 oz sultanas
1/2 tsp dried ginger
salt and pepper
1 tsp cornflour blended with water to thicken

Place the chicken in a non-metallic dish and add the rind and juice of the lemon, the sherry and stock, the sultanas and ginger, and a seasoning of salt and pepper. Leave to marinade somewhere cool for at least 1 hour.

Place the chicken and marinading ingredients in a flameproof casserole. Cover and bring to the boil. Transfer to a simmering oven for 1 1/2–2 hours. Thicken the sauce with the cornflour (see page 21) before serving.

Serves 4

CHICKEN IN COCONUT

The coconut gives this chicken a delicious creamy flavour, but also a grainy texture. If you like hot curries add more fresh chilli or use dried chillies instead.

4 tbsp vegetable oil
50g/2 oz desiccated coconut, soaked in a little water
3 fresh red chillies, seeded and chopped
2 tsp coriander seeds
1 cinnamon stick
1 tsp cumin seeds
8 black peppercorns
4 cloves
1/2 tsp ground turmeric
400ml/14 oz can coconut milk
5 cloves garlic, chopped
1 cube of fresh ginger about 2.5cm/1 inch square, chopped
2 onions, chopped
1kg/2 lb 4 oz chicken joints
salt

Heat about 1 tablespoon of oil in a frying pan. Drain the soaked coconut and fry in the oil. Drain and reserve. To the hot pan add the chillies, coriander, cinnamon, cumin seed, peppercorns, cloves, and turmeric. Stir for 1–2 minutes, adding more oil if necessary.

Put this mixture into a processor or blender with half the coconut milk, the garlic, ginger and half the onions. Blend to make a smooth paste.

Heat 3 tablespoons of oil in a flameproof casserole and sauté the remaining onions until soft. Add the spice mixture, sauté and then stir in the chicken. Add salt to taste and more coconut milk if necessary, to make a sauce. Cover, bring to the boil and transfer to a simmering oven for 3–4 hours.

Serves 4

BASQUE CHICKEN

....

This is a perfect casserole for my daughter who loves red peppers and olives. There are times of the year when red peppers become ridiculously expensive – at that time substitute green peppers or canned ones.

6 chicken portions
1 tbsp seasoned flour
1 tbsp olive oil
25g/1 oz butter
2 large onions, sliced
2 red peppers, seeded and sliced
100g/4 oz green olives
salt and pepper
225g/8 oz tomatoes, peeled and roughly chopped
300ml/1/2 pint chicken stock

Toss the chicken in the seasoned flour. Heat the oil and butter in a frying pan, and brown the chicken portions. Remove and place in a shallow casserole dish.

Add the onions, peppers and tomatoes to the frying pan and cook for about 10 minutes until softening. Season with salt and pepper Add the olives and pour over the chicken. Add enough stock to cover the chicken by three-quarters. Cover and bring to the boil. Transfer to a simmering oven for 1 1/2–2 hours until the chicken is tender. Thicken the sauce (see page 21) if necessary.

Serves 6

....

CHICKEN AND MUSHROOM LASAGNE

Most people I know love lasagne. This is a variation using chicken instead of the usual beef. The finished dish can be frozen before the final cooking stage. Thaw thoroughly before finally cooking.

1.3kg/3 lb oven-ready chicken
300ml/^{1}/$_2$ pint white wine
1 onion
trimmings from 1 leek
celery stalk
bay leaf
6 peppercorns
100g/4 oz butter
1 clove garlic, crushed
450g/1 lb mushrooms, trimmed and sliced
100g/4 oz plain flour
225g/8 oz Gruyère cheese, grated
300ml/^{1}/$_2$ pint single cream
3 tbsp pinenuts, (optional)
225g 8 oz ready-to-use lasagne
salt and pepper

Place the chicken in a large casserole. Add the wine, onion, leek trimmings, celery, bay leaf and peppercorns. Add enough water to come halfway up the chicken. Season with salt and pepper. Cover, bring to the boil and transfer to a simmering oven for 2^1/$_2$ hours until tender. Leave to cool a little.

Cut the chicken into bite-sized pieces, discarding the skin and bone. Strain the cooking liquor – you will need 1L/1^3/$_4$ pints. If necessary reduce by rapid boiling to the amount required.

Melt the butter in a saucepan and sauté the mushrooms and garlic for about 10 minutes until softened. Drain from the butter and set aside. Add the flour to the melted butter and whisk in the reserved cooking liquor. Bring to the boil. Off the heat stir in the single cream and half the Gruyère cheese.

Butter a shallow oven-proof dish well and pour a little sauce into the bottom. Lay on a layer of pasta followed by half the chicken and mushrooms. Add a little more sauce and then continue as before. Finish with a layer of lasagne. Pour on any remaining sauce and sprinkle over the remaining Gruyère and the pinenuts, if using. Place the shelf on the bottom set of runners of the top oven set to 'Bake' and slide in the prepared lasagne. Bake for 45–60 minutes until golden brown and cooked.

Serves 6

SWEET AND SOUR BARBECUED CHICKEN

....

This is a simple casserole dish that has a sweet–savoury taste. The chicken is tenderised by the flavoursome pineapple marinade.

825g/1 lb 13 oz can pineapple pieces, drained
bunch spring onions, trimmed and chopped
125ml/4 fl oz tomato ketchup
50ml/2 fl oz maple syrup
2 tbsp vinegar
juice 1/2 lemon
2 cloves garlic, crushed
salt and pepper
6 chicken quarters
3 tbsp vegetable oil

In a non-metallic bowl combine the pineapple, onions, tomato ketchup, maple syrup, vinegar, lemon juice, garlic, and salt and pepper. Mix well, then add the chicken, turning to coat well. Cover and leave to marinade in the fridge for 4–5 hours or overnight.

Scrape the marinade off the chicken. Heat the oil in a large frying pan, brown the chicken well and place in a casserole dish. Pour over the marinade, cover and bring to the boil. Transfer to a simmering oven, for 1½ hours, until the chicken is tender.

Serves 6

....

BRAISED CHICKEN AND CHICORY

Chicory is a much under-used vegetable. It is particularly nice braised and goes well with the chicken. The crème fraîche makes a creamy sauce.

25g/1 oz butter
2 tbsp oil
12 chicken thighs
3 heads chicory
3 teaspoons brown sugar
salt and pepper
6 shallots, finely chopped
juice 1½ lemons
200ml/8 fl oz dry white wine
250ml/9 fl oz crème fraîche
chopped parsley, to garnish

Heat the butter and oil in a frying pan and brown the chicken thighs. Drain and put in a casserole. Split the chicory heads lengthways and brown in the hot pan. Toss with the sugar and allow to caramelise a little. Add to the chicken and season with salt and pepper.

Sauté the shallots in the frying pan and when softened add the lemon juice and wine. Boil for 1-2 minutes and then whisk in the créme fraîche. Pour over the chicken, cover the casserole and gently bring to the boil on the hotplate.

Transfer to a simmering oven and cook for 1–1½ hours until the chicken is tender. Check the seasoning, garnish with parsley and serve.

Serves 6

DUCK BREASTS IN WHITE WINE

Many people think duck is a fatty meat. This method removes the fat, keeps the meat moist but still retains the delicious flavour of duck.

4 duck breasts
1 onion, sliced
1 large carrot sliced
1 celery stalk, sliced
300ml/1/2 pint dry white wine
salt and pepper
mashed potatoes, to serve

Remove the skin and attached layer of fat from the duck breasts. Place some of the skin fat in a flameproof casserole and heat until 2–3 tablespoons of fat run. Remove the skin and brown the meat on all sides. Remove from the pan.

Now sauté the vegetables in the hot fat until softening. Return the duck to the pan and pour in the wine. Bring to a fast boil, then season with salt and pepper.

Cover and place in a simmering oven, for 2–3 hours. Serve with lots of mashed potatoes to soak up the juices.

Serves 4

RABBIT IN THE DAIRY

This old English recipe has such a wonderful name that I couldn't resist trying it! This is a mild flavoured recipe, suitable for young or farmed rabbit. As there is very little colour in the finished dish, serve some brightly coloured fresh vegetables with it.

2 rabbits, jointed, or enough portions for 8
6 rashers bacon, rinded and diced
2 large onions, finely chopped
salt and pepper
a blade of mace or a pinch of ground mace
1.2L/2 pints milk
25g/1 oz cornflour

Wash and dry the rabbit, and place in a casserole dish. Add the bacon, onions, salt, pepper and mace. Pour over the milk, cover and bring to the boil. Transfer to a simmering oven and cook for 3 hours.

Remove the rabbit joints and keep warm. Blend the cornflour with a little milk or water and stir into the cooking liquid. Boil, stirring to thicken the sauce. Adjust the seasoning, pour over the rabbit and serve.

Serves 6–8

RABBIT WITH DIJON MUSTARD

Rabbit makes very good casserole meat and goes particularly well with mustard. If rabbit is not available, chicken may be substituted. Wild rabbit has much more flavour than farmed rabbit, if you have the choice.

1 tbsp olive oil
25g/1 oz butter
100g/1 lb rabbit joints
2 small onions, finely chopped
225g/8 oz mushrooms, sliced
2 tbsp brandy
150ml/1/4 pint chicken stock
150ml/1/4 pint double cream
4–6 tbsp Dijon mustard
salt and pepper
chopped parsley, to garnish

Heat the oil and butter in a frying pan and brown the rabbit pieces all over. Drain and transfer to a plate.

Soften the onions and mushrooms in the hot pan, then pour on the brandy, warm through and ignite. When the flames have died down pour in the chicken stock and whisk in the double cream. Simmer gently while you smear the mustard over the rabbit portions. Place these in a casserole dish pour over the sauce and season. Simmer gently, cover and transfer to a simmering oven for 1–1½ hours. Check the seasoning and serve sprinkled with chopped parsley.

Serves 4

HARE STEW WITH WHISKY

Jugged hare is a classic English dish, but few people have access to the necessary fresh hare and its blood. So this recipe is a modern adaptation. If hare is not available use rabbit, stewing venison and older game birds.

1 hare, jointed
25g/1 oz flour, seasoned with salt and paprika
50g/2 oz butter
100g/4 oz bacon, each rasher quartered
2 large onions, finely chopped
4 celery stalks, chopped
2 sprigs each thyme and mint
2 tsp Worcestershire sauce
150ml/¼ pint whisky
450ml/¾ pint stock, either from hare trimmings
or good beef stock

Coat the joints of hare with the seasoned flour. In a frying pan, heat the butter and bacon, and when the fat has run from the bacon add the hare joints. Fry until browned all over, then transfer the hare and bacon to a casserole dish.

Fry the onions until softened and then add the celery. Cook until the celery is softened and the onion is golden brown. Stir in the whiskey, stock and Worcestershire sauce. Bring to the boil and pour over the hare. Tuck in the fresh herbs, cover with a lid and bring back to the boil. Transfer to a simmering oven for about 4 hours.

Serves 6–8

PIGEON WITH RAISINS

....

Pigeon needs long, slow cooking to tenderise it – unless you know it is a young pigeon, in which case it can be roasted. Most recipes these days remove the breast meat and use the remaining meat and bones to make a stock. This recipe uses the whole bird, one per person.

50g/2 oz butter
3 tbsp olive oil
4 pigeons
100g/4 oz raisins, soaked in warm water for 30 minutes
4 large onions, thinly sliced
1/2 tsp paprika
salt and pepper

Heat the butter and oil in a frying pan, and brown the pigeons well all over. Transfer to a casserole dish. Cook the onions in the hot fat until soft and golden brown. Season with salt, pepper and paprika, and add to the pigeons along with the drained raisins. Cover with a well fitting lid or a sheet of foil. Heat gently on the hotplate for a few minutes before transferring to a simmering oven for about 3 hours.

Serves 4

....

PHEASANT WITH MUSHROOMS

A traditional way to cook jointed pheasants. The length of cooking time will depend upon the age of the birds. A larger cock bird should serve four, or two hen birds should serve six.

1 tbsp oil
50g/2 oz butter
2 onions, sliced
3 carrots, sliced
1 pheasant, jointed
1 tbsp brandy
a bouquet garni
450ml/³⁄4 pint red wine
salt and pepper
8 shallots, peeled
8 button mushrooms
2 tbsp double cream

Heat the oil and half the butter in a frying pan and sauté the onion and carrots until soft. Drain and place in a casserole dish. Brown the pheasant portions in the hot pan and when browned all over pour on the brandy. When the brandy is hot, ignite with a match. Allow the flames to die down then transfer the pheasant to a casserole dish.

Pour the wine into the frying pan and bring to the boil, scraping all the sediment from the base of the pan. Season and pour over the pheasant. Add the bouquet garni. Cover, bring to the boil and transfer to a simmering oven for 3–4 hours. Towards the end of cooking time, heat the remaining butter in a frying pan and fry the shallots and mushrooms until lightly golden brown. Drain the gravy from the casserole into a saucepan and boil to reduce. The gravy may be thickened (see page 21) if liked. Stir in the shallots, mushrooms and cream. Bubble gently for 2-3 minutes. Taste and adjust the seasoning. Pour over the pheasant.

Serves 4

NORMANDY POT-ROAST PHEASANT

This is a recipe for older pheasants that are not suitable for roasting. The bird can take up to 5 hours to become really tender in a simmering oven, but the long, slow cooking will be rewarded with a wonderfully intense flavour.

1 pheasant
25g/1 oz seasoned flour
50g/2 oz butter
2 onions, chopped
2 celery stalks, chopped
2 apples, peeled and cored
150ml/¼ pint stock
150ml/¼ pint dry cider
bouquet garni
150ml/¼ pint double cream
2 eating apples, cored, sliced and fried in butter, to garnish

Dust the pheasant with the flour. Melt the butter in a frying pan and brown the pheasant all over. Remove and put into a casserole dish. Fry the onion and celery in the remaining hot fat in the pan until softening, then add the apples.

Add any remaining flour to the frying pan and stir well. Gradually add the stock and the cider. Bring to the boil and pour over the pheasant. Add the bouquet garni, cover and return to the boil. Then transfer to a simmering oven for 4–5 hours, until tender.

When tender, strain off the sauce into a small saucepan. If necessary boil to reduce to a thick, glossy sauce. Stir in the cream and check the seasoning. Serve garnished with the fried apple slices.

Serves 4-6

VENISON AND BEEF CASSEROLE

Venison adds a richness to beef casserole and casseroling is a good method of cooking cheaper cuts for a special dish.

450g/1 lb stewing venison
450g/1 lb stewing beef
300ml/1/2 pint robust red wine
2 tbsp olive oil
bouquet garni
salt and pepper
2 onions, sliced
2 carrots, thickly sliced

Cut the venison and beef into large dice and place in a non-metallic dish. Pour on the red wine, olive oil and add the bouquet garni, seasoning with salt and pepper. Cover and leave in a cool place for 12 hours or overnight.

Skim some of the oil from the top of the marinade and heat in a flameproof casserole. Drain the meat from the marinade and brown in the hot oil. Drain and transfer to a plate. Toss the onion and carrot in the hot oil and brown lightly. Return the meat to the casserole and pour on the remaining marinade. Bring gently to the boil and simmer for 5 minutes before transferring to a simmering oven for 4 hours. If liked thicken the gravy before serving (see page 21).

Serves 6

LAMB CASSOULET

....

Traditionally, Cassoulet is a bean and meat stew from the Languedoc region of France but different regions use different meats. This is a fairly straightforward recipe using simple ingredients readily available. Cheap stewing lamb on the bone will give flavour and will be sweet and tender to eat.

225g/8 oz dried haricot beans
225g/8 oz piece green streaky bacon
1 onion, stuck with 4 cloves
1 carrot, sliced
2 cloves garlic, peeled
bouquet garni
salt and pepper
1kg/2 lb 2 oz stewing lamb
6 meaty sausages
1 tbsp olive oil
400g/14 oz can chopped tomatoes
1 tbsp tomato purée
50g/2 oz fresh breadcrumbs
50g/2 oz butter, melted

Soak the beans overnight, drain and put in a large casserole. Cut the bacon into large dice and add to the beans with the onion, carrot, garlic and bouquet garni. Barely cover with water and bring to the boil on the hotplate. Transfer to a simmering oven for 1 hour until the beans are just tender.

Season the meat and sausages. Heat the olive oil in a frying pan and brown the lamb and the sausages on all sides. Remove the casserole from the oven and stir in the tomatoes and tomato purée. Lay the lamb and sausages on top. Cover and bring back to the boil on the hotplate. Return to a simmering oven for 3–4 hours. Sprinkle the breadcrumbs over the meat, then pour over the melted butter. Return to the oven and cook, uncovered, for a further hour.

Serves 6

....

LAMB GOULASH

A lamb and paprika stew topped off with plain yoghurt to make a creamy sauce. Serve with noodles or creamy mashed potatoes.

1kg/2 lb 4 oz middle neck of lamb
50g/2 oz butter
2 onions, sliced
150ml /¹/₄ pint red wine
4 tsp paprika
2 tbsp tomato purée
salt
400g/14 oz can chopped tomatoes
6 tbsp plain yoghurt
chopped parsley, to garnish

Trim the lamb and cut into cubes. Heat the butter in a frying pan and brown the meat on all sides. Drain and put in a casserole dish. Add the onions to the pan and cook to soften. Sprinkle on the paprika and stir well, gradually adding the wine and the tomato purée. Season and pour over the lamb.

Add the tomatoes to the dish. Cover, bring to the boil and transfer to the simmering oven for about 2 hours. Just before serving, stir in the yoghurt and sprinkle with parsley.

Serves 6

TRADITIONAL GREEK MOUSSAKA

....

This must be the most well known of Greek dishes. Some people use cooked lamb instead of raw, but I prefer this cooked from scratch. Aubergines are usually used as the topping but if you prefer you can use sliced, part-cooked potatoes.

2 aubergines, sliced
salt
olive oil
1 large onion sliced
2 cloves garlic crushed
450g/1 lb minced lamb
400g/14 oz can chopped tomatoes
1 tbsp chopped fresh basil or 1 tsp dried oregano
freshly grated nutmeg
150ml/1/4 pint red wine or stock
pepper

Sauce
300ml/1/2 pint milk
25g/1 oz flour
25g/1 oz butter
salt and pepper
pinch ground cinnamon
1 egg, beaten

Place the sliced aubergines in a colander and sprinkle with salt. Leave for 30 minutes then pat dry. Heat a tablespoon of olive oil in a frying pan and fry the aubergines on both sides until golden brown. Drain on kitchen paper. You will probably need to add more oil with each batch.

Heat a little oil in a flameproof casserole and sauté the chopped onion. Add the garlic and meat, and brown the meat well. Add the tomatoes, basil or oregano, nutmeg, wine or stock, and salt and pepper. Cover, bring to the boil and then place in a simmering oven for 1–2 hours. The meat should be tender and the sauce thick.

In an ovenproof dish make a base layer of half the fried aubergines. Spoon on the cooked lamb and top off with the remaining aubergines.

For the sauce, put the milk, flour, butter, and salt and pepper in a saucepan, and whisk over a medium heat until a smooth, glossy sauce is formed. Whisk in the cinnamon and the egg. Pour over the top of the aubergines and bake in the top oven with the shelf on the bottom set of runners, for about 15 minutes until the sauce is fluffy and golden brown.

Serves 4

LAMB AND APRICOT CASSEROLE

The addition of the apricots make a rich lamb casserole. The saffron, although expensive, adds a golden colour and a distinctive flavour. Creamed potatoes or saffron rice go well as accompaniments.

2 tsp ground cumin
1 tsp cloves
1 sprig fresh thyme
4 cloves garlic, crushed
175ml/6 fl oz fresh orange juice
3 tbsp olive oil
1.5kg/3 lb 5 oz boneless diced lamb
175g/6 oz dried apricots
75g/3 oz raisins
1 tsp saffron strands
300 ml/1/2 pint dry sherry
90ml/3 fl oz wine vinegar
3 tbsp flour
450ml/3/4 pint light stock
salt and pepper

In a large bowl mix together the cumin, cloves, thyme, garlic, orange juice and olive oil. Add the diced lamb and stir well. Cover and leave in the fridge to marinate overnight or for at least 3 hours. In a basin combine the apricots, raisins, saffron, sherry and vinegar. Marinate overnight or for at least 3 hours. Skim the oil from the marinade and heat this in a frying pan. Brown the meat well and transfer to a casserole. Stir the flour into the remaining oil in the pan and cook for about a minute. Whisk in the stock to make a smooth sauce. Add the fruit to the casserole and pour the marinade into the sauce in the pan. Season with salt and pepper. Pour over the meat and fruit in the casserole dish. Bring the casserole to the boil on the hotplate and bubble for 5 minutes. Transfer to a simmering oven for 3–4 hours.

Serves 8

MADRAS LAMB CURRY

This curry can easily be made for a crowd. It is best made the day before it is needed and reheated for the fullest flavour.

1 small fresh coconut or 50g/2 oz desiccated coconut
2 fresh red chillies, seeded and chopped
3 tsp paprika
2.5cm/1 inch piece fresh ginger root, chopped
6 cloves garlic
3 tsp ground coriander
2 bay leaves
cinnamon stick
6 cloves
1 tsp cumin seeds and 1 tsp poppy seeds
3 tbsp vegetable oil
2 onions, chopped
1kg/2 lb 4 oz stewing lamb, diced
3 tomatoes, peeled and chopped

If using desiccated coconut, soak half of it in some water. Take half the fresh coconut or the remaining desiccated coconut and place in a blender or food processor with 225ml/8 fl oz water. Whizz and then strain. Reserve the liquid.

Strain the soaked dried coconut or take the remaining half of the fresh coconut and put in the processor with the chillies, paprika, ginger, garlic, coriander, bay leaves, cinnamon stick, cloves, cumin seeds and poppy seeds. Grind together to make a paste. Add a little water if necessary. Heat a flameproof casserole with the oil and sauté the onion. Stir in the spice paste and fry over a low heat for about 15 minutes, stirring and adding 2–3 tablespoons of water if necessary to prevent burning. Add the diced meat and fry to brown all over. Add the tomatoes and cook again for 4–5 minutes to soften the tomatoes. Season with salt and add the reserved coconut liquid. Cover, bring to the boil and transfer to a simmering oven for 4-5 hours.

Serves 6

LAMB CURRY WITH FRIED SPICES

This is more a flavoursome dish than a hot curry. If you like heat in your curry replace the green chillies with hot red ones. Don't be put off by the long list of ingredients – there is nothing outlandish!

2 tbsp vegetable oil
7.5cm/3 inch stick cinnamon
3 bayleaves
10 peppercorns
6 cloves
1 large onion, finely chopped
5cm/2 inch piece fresh ginger root, finely chopped
2 cloves garlic, crushed
2 green chillies, seeded and chopped
1 tsp salt
1kg/2 lb 4 oz boneless lamb, cut into chunks
1/2 tsp ground turmeric
1 1/2 tsp ground coriander
1 tsp chilli powder
1 tsp garam masala
200g/7 oz can chopped tomatoes
4 tbsp plain yoghurt
1 cup water
fresh coriander leaves, to garnish

Heat the oil in a roomy frying pan and fry first the cinnamon and bay leaves, then the peppercorns and cloves. Add the onions and sauté until soft and lightly coloured. Add the ginger, garlic, chillies and salt, stir well and continue to cook for a further 2–3 minutes. Transfer to a flameproof casserole dish.

Brown the lamb in the hot pan and then add the turmeric, coriander, chilli powder and garam masala, and stir well. Add the tomatoes and the water if the mixture seems dry.

Add the lamb to the casserole dish and bring to the boil over a gentle heat. Transfer to a simmering oven for 3–4 hours. Stir the yoghurt into the lamb and warm through. Garnish with coriander leaves and serve.

Serves 6

SHEPHERD'S PIE

This is a dish often made with left–over cooked meat, but I like to make a shepherd's pie with slowly cooked fresh minced lamb. The slow cooking ensures that the meat is always tender. Top it off with fluffy mashed potatoes.

1 tbsp oil or dripping
1 onion, finely chopped
450g/1 lb minced lamb
1 tbsp flour
salt and pepper
150ml/¼ pint brown stock
1 tsp chopped parsley
1 tsp Worcestershire sauce
450g/1 lb potatoes, cut into even sized chunks
25g/1 oz butter
1–2 tbsp milk

Heat the oil in an ovenproof casserole and fry the onion until softening. Stir in the lamb and fry until evenly browned. Stir in the flour and cook for 1–2 minutes. Season with salt and pepper, and add the stock, parsley and Worcestershire sauce. Cover and bring to the boil then transfer to a simmering oven for 1–2 hours.

Place the potatoes in a saucepan, add a pinch of salt and about 2.5cm/1 inch of water. Bring to the boil and boil for 1 minute. Drain the water off, cover and transfer to a simmering oven for 40–60 minutes. When soft, drain again and mash with the butter and milk.

Remove the meat from the oven and pour into an ovenproof dish. Top with the mashed potatoes. Bake in the middle of the top oven set to 'Bake' for 30–40 minutes until golden brown on the top and piping hot.

Serves 6

LANCASHIRE HOTPOT

This is a traditional English stew taking its name from the deep pot in which it was always made. Although it has simple ingredients the combination of meat on the bone and long, slow cooking gives a delicious homely flavour. The kidneys add richness but may be left out if they are not to your liking.

1 tbsp vegetable oil or dripping
8 middle neck lamb chops
4 lamb kidneys, cored and sliced
1kg/2 lb 4 oz potatoes, sliced
2 onions, sliced
salt and pepper
300ml/1/2 pint light stock

Heat the oil or dripping in a frying pan and fry the chops and kidneys over a high heat until golden brown.

Put a layer of potatoes in the bottom of a deep ovenproof dish, layer on some of the onion and then some of the fried meat. Continue layering up, seasoning as you go. Finish with a layer of potatoes. Pour over the stock. Cover and cook in a simmering oven for 4–6 hours. Thirty minutes before serving, remove the lid and transfer to the top oven set to 'Roast' or raise the oven temperature to brown the top of the potatoes.

Serves 4

SPICED LEG OF LAMB

The spices add a flavoursome skin to the lamb, without being over-powering. This method of cooking gives you delicious vegetables all in one dish along with the gravy. You may want to serve a green vegetable and baked or roast potatoes with the lamb.

2 tsp ground coriander
1 tsp ground cumin
1 tsp paprika
1 tsp salt
1/2 tsp freshly ground black pepper
1/2 tsp ground ginger
1.3kg/3 lb leg lamb
2 tbsp oil
1 large carrot, sliced
1 onion, sliced
2 celery stalks, sliced
150ml/1/4 pint stock
1 tsp tomato purée

Mix the spices together and rub into the leg of lamb. Place on a plate and leave in the fridge to marinate overnight.

In a large frying pan, heat the oil and soften the carrot, onion and celery. Drain the vegetables and transfer to the roasting tin. Brown the meat all over in the hot fat – do not let it become too brown or the spices will taste bitter. Place the meat on the vegetables. Combine the stock and tomato purée, and pour round the vegetables.

Slide the tin on the second set of runners from the bottom of the top oven set to 'Roast' and roast the lamb for 30 minutes, then transfer to the bottom oven or reduce top oven to 'Simmer' for 2½ hours. The juices may be thickened slightly (see page 21) or served as they are.

Serves 6

CARDAMOM LAMB

This is a gentle spicy lamb dish – not at all hot – but if you like you can increase the chilli powder.

35 green cardamom pods
6 tbsp vegetable oil
2 tsp freshly ground black pepper
1 tsp ground turmeric
1 tsp chilli powder
1kg/2 lb 4 oz lamb meat, diced
150g/5 oz thick plain yoghurt
2 tsp ground coriander
3 tomatoes, peeled and chopped
salt

Place the cardamom pods in a processor or grinder and grind until fairly fine. Mix with a little water to make a paste.

Heat the oil in a flameproof casserole, add the cardamon paste and the pepper. Stir-fry for 2-3 minutes then add the turmeric, chilli powder and coriander, and stir in the meat. Cook over a medium heat, stirring, to cook the spices and prevent the meat sticking to the pan.

Add the yoghurt, tomatoes and a seasoning of salt. Stir well and then add about 300ml/½ pint water. Cover, bring to the boil and then transfer to a simmering oven for 4–5 hours.

Serves 6

SPRING LAMB

This is a delicate lamb casserole that suits the combination of spring lamb and baby new vegetables. If you can, choose small, evenly sized carrots as these will make the finished dish more attractive.

4 double cutlets of lamb
salt and pepper
25g/1 oz butter
2 small onions, finely sliced
300ml/½ pint stock
225g/8 oz young carrots, scraped and trimmed
450g/1 lb small, new potatoes, scrubbed

Trim the chops, cutting off excess fat. Season with salt and pepper. Melt the butter in a frying pan and brown the cutlets. Place in a shallow casserole dish. Add the onions to the hot frying pan and cook until soft. Add to the meat and pour on enough stock to barely cover the cutlets.

Place the prepared potatoes and carrots round the meat. Cover and slowly bring to the boil. Transfer to a simmering oven and cook for 1½–2 hours until the meat and vegetables are cooked.

Serves 4

NAVARIN OF LAMB

....

This is a springtime recipe incorporating tender spring vegetables that give a bright appearance to the finished dish.

3 tbsp olive oil
1kg/2 lb 4 oz boned shoulder of lamb, cut into large dice
100g/4 oz each onion, celery and carrot, cut into large dice
2 cloves garlic, crushed
2tbsp tomato purée
1 tbsp flour
150ml/1/4 pint dry white wine
2 bay leaves
sprig of fresh thyme
1L/13/4 pints stock
100g/4 oz small carrots
150g/6 oz small new potatoes
1 tbsp caster sugar
25g/1 oz butter
100g/4 oz each of asparagus and French beans
salt and pepper

Heat the oil in a large frying pan and brown the meat in batches, transferring to a casserole. Fry the onion, celery and carrot until softening. Add the garlic, tomato purée and flour and stir well. Slowly add the wine and bubble until reduced by half. Add to the lamb along with the bay leaves, thyme and stock. Bring to the boil over a gentle heat and transfer to a simmering oven for 1½–2 hours. Trim the small carrots and new potatoes. Put the sugar, butter, 150ml/5 fl oz water, carrots and potatoes in a saucepan. Bring to the boil and transfer, uncovered, to a simmering oven for 15 minutes. At this point the vegetables should be glazed. Remove the lamb from the casserole to a plate. Discard the bay leaves and thyme. Purée the gravy and vegetables left in the casserole. Cook the beans and asparagus in a little fast-boiling water for 3–4 minutes. Combine the lamb and sauce, and season to taste. Add the potatoes, carrots, beans and asparagus.

Serves 6

....

....

LAMB COUSCOUS

This is a complete meal on a plate – however there is some last-minute work to be done! Adding the vegetables to the lamb and preparing the couscous will take about 30 minutes. Harissa is a spicy Moroccan chilli paste, available from most supermarkets and specialist food shops.

50g/2 oz butter
1 clove garlic, crushed
2 onions, chopped
1 red chilli, chopped
2 bay leaves
1 tsp ground cumin
1/2 tsp freshly ground black pepper
1/2 tsp ground ginger
1 cinnamon stick
450g/1 lb lamb, diced
400g/14 oz can chick-peas, drained
2 each carrots, small turnips and courgettes,
trimmed and quartered.
4 tomatoes, peeled and quartered
1 small aubergine, diced
3 tbsp chopped fresh coriander
3 tbsp chopped parsley
450ml/3/4 pint light stock
225g/8 oz couscous
50g/2 oz butter
salt and pepper
harissa (optional)

Heat the butter over a low heat in a flameproof casserole and stir in the garlic, onions, chilli, bay leaves, cumin, pepper, ginger and cinnamon stick. Fry for 1-2 minutes. Add the lamb and chick-peas, and enough water to half cover the lamb. Cover and bring to the boil. Transfer to a simmering oven for 2 hours. Add the prepared vegetables and herbs to the lamb, bring to the boil again and return to a simmering oven for a further 20-30 minutes until the vegetables are cooked.

Bring the stock to the boil in a saucepan, stir in the couscous. Remove from the heat and cover. Stand for 20 minutes, then stir in the butter. Check seasoning and serve with the lamb. To add a little more heat and an authentic flavour, accompany this wonderful dish with a small bowl of harissa.

Serves 4

CIDER PORK WITH APPLES

....

Pork and apples always go well together. Use red-skinned apples to add colour to the finished dish.

1kg/2 lb 4 oz pork shoulder, cut into large dice
1 tbsp seasoned flour
3 tbsp oil
2 large onions, cut into eighths
300ml/½ pint cider
300ml/½ pint light stock
salt and pepper
2 red-skinned eating apples

Toss the meat in the seasoned flour. Heat the oil in a frying pan and brown the meat in batches. Transfer to a casserole dish. Add the onions to the frying pan, gently fry until softening and golden brown. Add to the meat.

Stir the cider and stock into the frying pan, season with salt and pepper and bring to the boil, scraping up all the residue from the base of the pan. Pour over the meat in the casserole. Place the casserole on the hotplate, cover and bring to the boil. Transfer to a simmering oven and cook for 1 hour.

Quarter and core the apples and add to the casserole and cook for another 30–40 minutes until the meat and apples are tender, but not falling apart.

Serves 6

....

SOMERSET CIDER HOTPOT

I like to make this with pork, but veal or even pieces of bacon joint also work well with this meal-in-a-pot.

675g/1 lb 8 oz pork, cubed
1 tbsp seasoned flour
2 tbsp vegetable oil
675g/1 lb 8 oz potatoes, thickly sliced
450g/1 lb leeks, trimmed and sliced
salt and pepper
450ml/3/4 pint Somerset cider
2 tbsp tomato purée

Coat the meat with seasoned flour. Heat the oil in a frying pan and brown the meat all over.

Lay some potatoes in the base of the casserole dish and then a layer of leeks, seasoning each layer with salt and pepper. Put in the browned meat, then more leeks and finish with a layer of potatoes.

Mix together the cider and tomato purée, and pour over the potatoes. Cover, bring to the boil and transfer to a simmering oven for 3–4 hours. Remove the lid and brown off in the top of the oven with the temperature rising to 'Bake' for 30 minutes.

Serves 4

NEW ORLEANS CAJUN PORK

This is a flavoursome way to cook pork that has the added bonus of looking attractive on the plate with a range of bright colours. It is best served with couscous or rice.

1 kg/2 lb 4 oz diced shoulder pork
4 green chillies, seeded and finely chopped
4 cloves garlic, crushed
1/4 tsp cayenne pepper
1 tbsp Cajun seasoning
2 tbsp vegetable oil
2 large onions, peeled and cut into wedges
1 red pepper, seeded and cut into large squares
1 yellow pepper, seeded and cut onto large squares
400g/14 oz can plum tomatoes
150ml/1/4 pint chicken stock
2–3 sprigs fresh thyme
salt and pepper

Place the pork, chillies, garlic, cayenne and Cajun seasoning in a bowl and mix well. Cover and leave in the fridge overnight.

Heat the oil in a frying pan and fry the pork until a deep golden brown. Transfer to a casserole dish. Add the onions and peppers to the frying pan and cook for 5 minutes until just starting to colour and soften. Add to the pork. Stir in the remaining ingredients and season with salt and pepper.

Place the casserole on the hotplate and bring gently to the boil. Transfer to a simmering oven for 3–4 hours.

Serves 6

PORK WITH HONEY AND APRICOTS

Pork and fruit always work well together. Dried apricots add a delicious flavour and texture – slightly Middle Eastern. Serve with couscous or mashed potatoes.

1kg/2 lb 4 oz boneless pork, diced
2 tbsp seasoned flour
2 tbsp vegetable oil
2 onions, chopped
100g/4 oz dried apricots
salt and pepper
2 tbsp honey
600ml/1 pint light stock
1 cinnamon stick

Toss the pork in the seasoned flour. Heat the oil in a frying pan and brown the prepared meat. Transfer to a casserole dish.

Add the onions to the hot frying pan and sauté until softening and a pale golden colour. Stir in the apricots, salt and pepper to taste, honey and stock. Bring to the boil and pour over the meat. Add the cinnamon stick and cover. Bring to the boil. Place in a simmering oven for 3–4 hours.

Serves 6

PORK WITH RED WINE AND PRUNES

....

The addition of prunes, redcurrant jelly and red wine gives a rich sauce to this pork casserole. Serve with mashed potatoes to absorb the rich gravy.

2kgs/4 lb 8 oz boneless shoulder of pork, diced
2 tbsp seasoned flour
2 tbsp vegetable oil
2 onions, sliced
1/2 bottle red wine
300ml/1/2 pint light stock
225g/8 oz redcurrant jelly
225g/8 oz ready-to-eat prunes
a few sprigs thyme
2–3 sage leaves

Toss the pork in the seasoned flour. Heat the oil in a frying pan and brown the meat in batches. Transfer each batch to a large casserole dish.

Cook the onions in the frying pan until softening, pour in the wine and bring to the boil. Add the stock and redcurrant jelly, stirring to dissolve the jelly, and add the prunes. Pour the hot liquid over the meat in the casserole and add the herbs. Bring to the boil and transfer to a simmering oven for 2 hours.

Serves 8

....

PORK CASSEROLE WITH HERB DUMPLINGS

....

1kg/2lb 4oz pork shoulder steaks
2 tbsp seasoned flour
2 tbsp vegetable oil
2 onions, 2 large carrots, sliced
4 celery stalks, chopped
600ml/1 pint light stock
1 bouquet garni
salt and pepper

Dumplings
100g/4 oz self-raising flour
100g/4 oz fresh breadcrumbs
100g/4 oz shredded suet
salt and pepper
1/2 tsp, dried mixed herbs or 1 tbsp chopped fresh mixed herbs

Toss the pork in the seasoned flour. Heat the oil in a frying pan and brown the meat on all sides. Transfer to a casserole dish. Add the onion, celery and carrot to the pan and sauté until softening. Pour in the stock and bring to the boil. Pour the mixture over the meat and add the bouquet garni and a seasoning of salt and pepper. Cover and bring to the boil. Transfer to a simmering oven for about 4 hours.

Raise the top oven temperature to 'Bake'. Prepare the dumplings. In a mixing bowl mix together the flour, breadcrumbs, suet, salt, pepper and herbs. Blend together with enough cold water to make a stiff dough. Shape into 12 dumplings. Place the dumplings on the top of the meat, so that the base is sitting in the gravy. Transfer the casserole to the middle set of runners of the top oven, and cook for a further 20–30 minutes.

Serves 6

....

SCRUMMY SAUSAGES

....

Most children like sausages, pasta and tomato sauce, so this way of cooking sausages and serving with pasta is usually a winner.

3 tbsp olive oil
2 large onions, finely chopped
2 cloves garlic, crushed
1 large red chilli, seeded and finely chopped
2 x 400g/14 oz cans chopped tomatoes
1 tsp sugar
salt and pepper
8 thick sausages
3 tbsp seasoned flour
pasta shapes, to serve

In a flameproof casserole heat 1 tablespoon of the oil and fry the onion, garlic and chilli until soft. Add the tomatoes, sugar, and salt and pepper. Bring to the boil and transfer, uncovered, to a simmering oven for at least an hour until a thick sauce has formed.

Skin the sausages and cut each one into three. Roll each portion into a ball and roll to coat in the flour. Heat the remaining 2 tablespoons of oil in a frying pan and brown the sausage balls until golden brown all over. Add to the tomato sauce, bring to the boil and then return to a simmering oven for 30 minutes. Serve with pasta shapes.

Serves 6

....

BOSTON BAKED BEANS

This is a classic American recipe, although the beans in this recipe bear no resemblance to the canned variety! The treacle gives a dark colour and a distinctive sweetness. Sausages browned in a frying pan can be added for the last hour to make a substantial one-pot meal.

225g/8 oz dried cannellini beans
bouquet garni
500ml/18 fl oz vegetable stock
450g/1 lb belly pork
1 leek, finely sliced
1 carrot, sliced
1 onion, quartered
2 tbsp black treacle
2 tsp strong mustard
2 tbsp soft brown sugar
salt and pepper

Pick over the dried beans and place in a bowl. Cover with cold water and soak overnight. Drain, rinse and put in a saucepan. Add the bouquet garni and enough stock to just cover the beans. Cover, bring to the boil, then transfer to a simmering oven for 1 hour until just tender. Drain, reserving the cooking water.

Chop the pork into large cubes and put half in the base of a casserole dish. Add the beans and the prepared vegetables and then the remaining meat. Mix together the treacle, mustard and sugar, add to the casserole and season to taste. Pour in enough of the bean cooking water to almost cover the ingredients. Cover and gently bring to the boil on the hotplate, then transfer to a simmering oven for 6 hours. Check the seasoning before serving.

Serves 4–6

VEAL GOULASH

Stewing veal is readily available in butchers shops and supermarkets. It makes a tasty stew.

1kg/2 lb 4 oz stewing veal
1 tbsp flour
25g/1 oz butter
1 tbsp vegetable oil
1 onion, sliced
2 carrots, sliced
150ml/1/4 pint white wine
1 tbsp paprika
1/2 tsp cayenne pepper
1 tbsp tomato purée
450ml/3/4 pint light stock
salt

Toss the meat in the flour. Heat the butter and oil in a frying pan and brown the meat all over. Transfer to a casserole dish.

Add the onion and carrots to the pan, sauté, then add to the meat. Pour the wine into the hot pan and scrape off all the residue from the base of the pan. Stir in the paprika, cayenne, tomato purée and the stock, and bring to the boil. Lightly season with salt.

Pour the liquid over the meat, cover, bring to the boil and transfer to the simmering oven for 2–3 hours. Check seasoning before serving.

Serves 6

CASEROLE OF VEAL

....

350g/12 oz shoulder of veal, boned and cut into strips
75g/3 oz butter
2 onions, sliced
3 carrots, sliced
1 clove garlic, crushed
25g/1 oz seasoned flour
300ml/1/2 pint veal or chicken stock
4 tomatoes, peeled, seeded and chopped
4 celery stalks, chopped
salt and pepper

Toss the veal in the seasoned flour. Heat the butter in a frying pan and brown the meat in this. Drain and transfer to a casserole dish. Add the onions and carrots to the hot butter and fry until softening. Add the garlic and any remaining flour. Cook for 1–2 minutes, then gradually stir in the stock. Bring to the boil, then add the tomatoes and celery. Simmer for 1–2 minutes and add to the veal. Season to taste, cover and bring back to the boil. Transfer to a simmering oven for 2 hours.

Serves 4

....

OSSO BUCO

....

This is a classic Italian dish using veal that is cooked gently in a tomato sauce. The sauce becomes rich from the slow cooking and the marrow in the bones. Serve with a rissotto or creamy mashed potatoes.

4 pieces osso buco shin of veal
salt and pepper
1 tbsp plain flour
2 tbsp olive oil
1 onion, finely chopped
1 clove garlic, crushed
1 carrot, diced
1 celery stalk, finely sliced
1 leek, finely sliced
50g/2 oz peeled and diced celeriac
1 tbsp chopped basil
2 tomatoes, peeled and chopped
2 tbsp tomato purée
150ml/1/4 pint dry white wine
600ml/1 pint beef stock

Season the osso buco with salt and pepper, and lightly dust with flour. Heat the oil in a frying pan and brown the meat well on both sides. Transfer to a casserole dish large enough to take all the meat pieces in one layer.

Sauté the onion, garlic, carrot, celery, leek and celeriac for a few minutes in the hot pan, until the vegetables are softening. Stir in the basil, tomatoes, tomato paste and the wine. Stir well and bubble until reduced by half. Add the stock and again boil well, then pour over the osso buco. Cover, return to the boil, then place in a simmering oven, until the veal is tender and the sauce is thick. Check the seasoning before serving.

Serves 4

....

VEGETABLE CURRY

....

A warming winter dish best made when there is a plentiful supply of root vegetables. You can substitute the vegetables listed but do not overdo the variety or you will lose the individual flavours. Cut the vegetables large enough to give a good appearance and bite to the curry.

2 cloves garlic, peeled
2.5cm/1 inch cube fresh ginger root, grated
2 tsp each coriander seeds and cumin seeds
1 tsp each mustard seeds and cardamom seeeds
10 cloves
1 stick cinnamon, about 7.5cm/3 inches
1 tsp cayenne pepper, 1 tsp ground turmeric
75g/3 oz clarified butter, ghee or vegetable oil
400ml/14 fl oz can coconut milk
juice 1 lemon
2 large parsnips, chopped
½ small cauliflower, broken into florets
100g 4 oz button mushrooms, wiped
a large head broccoli, cut into portions
4 potatoes, cut into chunks
1 large onion, sliced
4 carrots, chopped
1 tsp salt

Put the garlic and ginger in a mortar or small processor and grind to make a paste. Grind the whole spices to a powder, then mix with the cayenne and turmeric. In a flameproof casserole heat the butter and sauté the onion, garlic and ginger until the onion is golden brown. Add the salt and spices, and cook for 1–2 minutes. Add the carrots, coconut milk and lemon juice. Bring to the boil and then add the parsnips, cauliflower, mushrooms and potatoes. Cover and transfer to a simmering oven for about 1 hour, until the vegetables are tender, but not mushy. Remove the casserole from the oven and stir in the broccoli. Cook quickly on the hotplate to retain the bright colour. Taste and adjust the seasoning.

Serves 6

....

PROVENÇAL BEAN STEW

This is a two-stage dish, in that the beans need to be cooked before adding to the remaining ingredients. This makes a good main course dish served with crispy salad and good bread to mop up any juices.

350g/12 oz haricot beans, soaked overnight
2 tbsp olive oil
1 onion, sliced
1 red pepper, seeded and sliced
1 green pepper, seeded and sliced
2 cloves garlic, crushed
400g/14 oz can chopped tomatoes
2 tbsp tomato purée
salt and pepper
12 black olives, pitted
10 basil leaves, shredded

Drain the beans, place in a flameproof casserole and cover with cold water. Cover and bring to the boil, then transfer to a simmering oven for 2–3 hours. Drain and set aside.

In the casserole, heat the oil and sauté the onion, red and green peppers and garlic until softening, but not brown. Add the tomatoes, tomato purée and some salt and pepper. Stir in the cooked beans, bring gently to the boil and transfer to a simmering oven for 1–1½ hours. Stir in the olives and sprinkle with basil.

Serves 4

ACCOMPANIMENTS

ACCOMPANIMENTS

Casseroles and stews out of a simmering oven deserve a good accompaniment. The easiest, of course, are jacket potatoes, deservedly one thing that new Rayburn owners rave about, with their crispy skins and fluffy insides.

If the main dish has a lot of gravy choose a starchy accompaniment that will absorb some of the juices. Rice goes well with curries, and couscous with fruity Mediterranean dishes, but they can, of course, be used with other dishes or even as salads. The list is endless, here are just a few ideas.

POLENTA

This is an everyday food in Northern Italy, so with the increase in Italian foods being eaten in this coutry it is not surprising to see polenta widely available in the supermarkets. Served hot and wet it is a good accompaniment to casseroles and stews. Allowed to set and then grilled or fried, it goes well with drier food and salads. If you buy ready-cooked or quick-cook polenta then follow the instructions on the packet.

250g/9 oz polenta
1.2L/2 pints water
salt and pepper
100g/4 oz butter
75g/3 oz freshly grated Parmesan cheese (optional)
olive oil

Pour the polenta into a jug. Measure the water into a saucepan and bring to the boil. Transfer to the simmering plate and stir in the polenta in a steady stream, beating well. Cook over a gentle heat, stirring vigorously and frequently until the polenta comes away from the sides of the pan. Season with salt and pepper.

Stir the butter, and cheese if using, into the hot polenta at once. Serve.

If you wish to serve the polenta grilled or fried, pour on to a shallow plate or baking tray and allow to cool and set. To grill or fry, cut into portions and brush with olive oil. Then grill or fry until golden brown.

Serves 4

DUMPLINGS

Small dumplings are used to finish off stews and casseroles. Once the dumplings have been added to the casserole move the dish to a hot oven for the final cooking time. They are a delicious way of soaking up the gravy.

HERB AND HORSERADISH DUMPLINGS FOR BEEF STEWS

100g/4 oz self-raising flour
100g/4 oz white breadcrumbs
50g/2 oz shredded suet
2 tbsp chopped mixed herbs
2 tsp horseradish sauce
salt and pepper
1 or 2 eggs, beaten

Mix together the flour, breadcrumbs, suet and herbs. Add the horseradish, salt and pepper. Stir in enough beaten egg, to make a soft dough. Divide into 16 dumplings. Place on top of the stew for the last 30 minutes of the cooking time.

PARSLEY DUMPLINGS FOR VEAL, LAMB AND CHICKEN

175g/6 oz fresh breadcrumbs
75g/3 oz shredded suet
2 tbsp chopped parsley
grated rind 1/2 lemon
salt and pepper
1 or 2 eggs, beaten

Mix together the breadcrumbs, suet, parsley, lemon rind, and salt and pepper. Stir in enough beaten egg to make a soft dough. Put spoonfuls of the dough on top of the casserole for the last 15–20 minutes.

SUET DUMPLINGS

These are always associated with beef stews. Ring the changes with flavourings such as mustard, chopped mint or sorrel.

225g/8 oz plain flour
1/2 tsp baking powder
salt
100g/4 oz shredded suet

Sieve the flour, baking powder and salt into a basin. Mix in the suet and bind together with cold water to make a stiff dough. Shape into 16 dumplings and cook for 20 minutes on top of the casserole.

RED CABBAGE WITH APPLE

Red cabbage is delicious with rich meats such as pork or game. I like any left-overs cold as a salad.

1 small red cabbage
1 cooking apple, peeled, cored and thickly sliced
1 small onion, thinly sliced
25g/1 oz butter
salt and pepper
1 tbsp redcurrant jelly (optional)

Shred the cabbage finely – this can be done either in a food processor or with a sharp knife. Place in a flameproof casserole with the apple, onion and butter. Season with salt and pepper and toss well to mix. Cover and heat gently on the hotplate until the butter has melted. Place in a simmering oven for about 2 hours. If you like, add a tablespoon of redcurrant jelly before serving.

Serves 4-6

POTATO AND APPLE MASH

This is a favourite mashed potato recipe to go with sausages and pork.

To every 450g/1 lb of potatoes use one cooking apple. Peel the potatoes and cut into large chunks. Peel, quarter and core the apples. Put together in a saucepan with about 2.5cm/1 inch water. Cover and bring to the boil on the hotplate, and boil for 1 minute. Drain and replace the lid. Transfer to a simmering oven for about an hour or until the potatoes are soft enough to mash. Drain off any excess moisture and mash the apples and potatoes with butter until smooth. Season with salt and pepper. Grate a red-skinned apple, leaving the skin on, and fold into the mash. This gives an attractive appearance.

MASHED SWEDE

Swede can be very dull as a boiled vegetable, but cooked this way it is delicious.

Peel the swede, cut into large chunks and place in a saucepan with 2.5cm/1 inch water and a pinch of salt. Cover and bring to the boil on the hotplate and boil for 1 minute. Drain the water from the pan and replace the lid. Transfer to a simmering oven for 1–1½ hours. When the swede is soft enough to mash, drain the water. Mash or purée the swede with plenty of butter and a generous grating of nutmeg. Taste and season with salt if needed.

GARLIC MASHED POTATOES

A favourite with my publisher! Olive oil can be used to mash the potatoes, but personally I prefer butter.

450g/1 lb maincrop potatoes
salt
4 cloves garlic, peeled
50g/2 oz butter or 2–3 tsp olive oil
pepper

Place the potatoes in a saucepan with about 2.5cm/1inch water, a good pinch of salt and the garlic cloves. Cover and bring to the boil. Boil for 1 minute and then drain off the water. Re-cover and place the pan in a simmering oven for 40–60 minutes until the potatoes are soft enough to mash. Drain off any excess moisture and mash the potatoes and garlic with the butter and some pepper.

Serves 4

PARSNIP PURÉE

Parsnips are one of my favourite winter vegetables. Those baby ones in the supermarket in the summer have no flavour, so keep this as a winter dish to go with hearty roasts and warming casseroles.

Peel and cut the parsnips into large chunks. Place in a saucepan with about 2.5cm/1 inch water and a pinch of salt. Cover and bring to the boil on the boiling plate. Boil for 1 minute and then drain off the water. Cover and transfer to a simmering oven until the parsnips are soft enough to mash. This may take 1–1 ½ hours, depending on the age of the parsnips. Drain any excess moisture and then mash or purée the parsnips with butter, salt and pepper, a pinch of cinnamon and a little chopped parsley.

CELERIAC PURÉE

Although this has the flavour of celery it is a totally different vegetable. Unless you grow your own it tends to be fairly expensive, so I usually mix it with potatoes, which absorb the strong flavour well.

Peel and cut into large chunks the potatoes and celeriac – about equal quantities of each vegetable. Place in a saucepan with 2. 5cm/1 inch water and a pinch of salt. Bring to the boil on the hotplate and boil for 1 minute before draining off the water. Cover and transfer to a simmering oven until the vegetables are soft enough to mash – about 1 hour. Drain off any excess moisture and then mash with a good knob of butter, some hot milk or cream, and a seasoning of salt and pepper.

FLAGEOLET BEAN SALAD

These dried green beans are probably the family favourite. They are a good ingredient for a mixed bean salad. This recipe can have salami pieces added to make the salad a meal in itself.

250g/8 oz dried flageolet beans, soaked overnight
salt and pepper
1 clove garlic, crushed
6 tbsp olive oil
3 tbsp white wine vinegar
1/4 tsp French mustard
pinch sugar
1 spring onion, finely chopped

Drain the beans and cover with fresh water in a flameproof casserole. Bring to the boil and transfer to a simmering oven for 1 1/2 –2 hours, until cooked but not mushy. Drain and transfer to a serving dish.

Place the remaining ingredients in a jam jar and shake well. Pour over the drained beans and stir well.

BUTTER BEAN VINAIGRETTE

For many years butter beans were my least favourite bean having had too many mushy ones at school! This recipe converted me, and my family likes them too!

250g/8 oz butter beans, soaked overnight
3 tbsp olive oil
1 tbsp wine vinegar
salt and pepper
4 spring onions, finely chopped
1 clove garlic, crushed
chopped parsley, to garnish

Rinse the beans and place in a flameproof casserole. Cover with water and bring to the boil. Cover and place in a simmering oven for $1\frac{1}{2}$–2 hours until the beans are cooked, but not mushy. Drain and transfer to a serving dish.

Place the oil, vinegar, and salt and pepper in a clean jam jar. Shake well and pour over the warm, beans. Add the onions and garlic and mix well, taking care not to break up the beans. Leave until cold, then sprinkle with chopped parsley to serve.

Serves 4–6

PUY LENTILS

....

The advantage of lentils is that they need no soaking. These little brown lentils have a lovely texture and nutty flavour. Serve this dish warm or cold as an accompaniment to other dishes or in a salad selection.

225g/8 oz Puy lentils, washed thoroughly
6 cloves garlic, unpeeled and cut in half
juice of 1 lemon
3 tbsp olive oil
2 tbsp chopped herbs, whatever is handy
salt and pepper

Place the lentils and garlic in a saucepan or flameproof casserole. Cover with water and bring to the boil. Cover and transfer to a simmering oven for 30–60 minutes until soft but still with some bite. Drain the lentils and discard the garlic. Mix together the lemon juice and olive oil, and pour over the lentils. Stir in the herbs and season with salt and pepper. Serve warm or cold.

Serves 6

....

COUSCOUS

....

Couscous is a staple from North Africa. The grain is made from semolina. It can be eaten as a salad or as an accompaniment for meat stews.

225g/8 oz couscous
450ml/³/₄ pint stock

Bring the stock to boil in a saucepan, then stir in the couscous. Remove from the heat and stand at the back of the Rayburn, covered. Leave to stand for 20 minutes. Fork through to fluff up and, if liked, stir in some butter, olive oil or vinaigrette dressing, depending upon what you are serving the couscous with.

....

SPICY CHICK-PEAS

Chick-peas are a useful source of protein for vegetarians, but they also make a delicious vegetable dish, either hot or cold.

225g/8 oz dried chick-peas, soaked overnight in cold water
2.5cm/1 inch cube fresh ginger root
1 green chilli, seeded and chopped
2 cloves garlic, peeled
2 tbsp vegetable oil or ghee
1 onion, chopped
½ tsp cumin seeds, crushed
1 tsp coriander seeds, crushed
1 tsp chilli powder
½ tsp ground turmeric
4 tomatoes, peeled and chopped
juice ½ lemon
salt and pepper

Drain the chick-peas and place in a large pan. Cover with water and bring to the boil, covered. Transfer to a simmering oven for about 2 hours, until tender. Drain and reserve the liquid.

Pound the ginger, chillis, and garlic together to make a paste, using either a mortar or processor. Heat the oil in a frying pan and sauté the onion until soft. Stir in the chilli paste, the crushed seeds, the chilli powder and turmeric, and cook for 1–2 minutes. Add the tomatoes and lemon juice. Stir into the chick-peas and moisten with some of the cooking liquid if the beans seem dry. Heat through in a simmering oven for 30 minutes, check the seasoning and serve hot or cold.

Serves 6

RATATOUILLE

....

This Mediterranean vegetable stew has been popular for years. The fashion now is to have a barely cooked selection of vegetables, but I still like a slow cooked stew. This is a versatile dish to serve on its own, as an accompaniment to simplycooked food, topped with cheese, cold as a salad or as a basis of a vegetable lasagne.

3 tbsp olive oil
2 cloves garlic, crushed
1 bay leaf
sprig of rosemary or thyme
2 onions, chopped
2 peppers, colour of choice, seeded and cut into large dice
2 courgettes, trimmed and sliced
450g/1 lb firm, ripe tomatoes, peeled, seeded and roughly chopped
1 aubergine, trimmed and cut into large dice
salt and pepper

Heat the oil in a flameproof casserole along with the garlic and herbs. Sauté the onions in the oil until softening but not browning. Drain and put to one side.

Now sauté the remaining vegetables in turn, then return them all to the pan, season and toss. Cover, heat through and transfer to a simmering oven for 1 hour until the vegetables are cooked but not mushy.

Serves 4–6

....

JACKET POTATOES

Scrub the potatoes well and cut a cross on one side of the potato. Place the potatoes on the oven shelf in the top oven set to 'Bake' or 'Roast' and bake for 1–1½ hours until crisp on the outside and fluffy in the middle.

The fillings listed below can be used either as a topping for the potatoes or the inside can be scooped out and mixed together with the chosen filling.

Fillings

Grated hard cheese such as Cheddar, Red Leicester or Gruyère

Slices of soft Brie mixed with chopped walnuts

Poached smoked haddock or salmon mixed with soured cream and parsley

Canned tuna fish, chopped chives and mayonnaise, mashed lightly together

Soured cream and crushed garlic

Fromage frais

Butter and crispy fried bacon

Butter and crispy fried onion rings

Sliced mushrooms sautéd in butter and mixed with thick yoghurt

Blue cheese crumbled into soured cream

PUDDINGS

PUDDINGS

The best puddings cooked slowly are steamed puddings – here the variety is almost endless. A quickly prepared pudding can be made from a basic all-in-one sponge mixture and topped off with jam or syrup. Here I am giving one or two slightly more exotic variations on the everyday steamed pudding. Remember that if you are not ready to serve the pudding at the time planned it will not spoil – 1–2 hours extra cooking is quite safe! The steaming on the hotplate is important to get a light, fluffy sponge. Allow extra cooking time if you know your oven cooks very slowly.

I have also added a selection of recipes for other puddings which benefit from slow cooking. Meringues in particular are suitable for slow cooking in the Rayburn's slow oven. They can even be left in overnight!

STEAMED ORANGE SPONGE

A light orange sponge served with an orange sauce. If you can, use frozen concentrated orange juice for a deep flavour.

100g/4 oz butter, softened
125g/4¹/₂ oz castor sugar
2 eggs, beaten
1 egg yolk
200g/7 oz self-raising flour
finely grated rind 1 orange
150ml/¹/₄ pint concentrated orange juice
Orange Sauce (see below) or cream, to serve

Cream together the butter and the sugar. Beat together the eggs and yolk, and beat into the creamed mixture. Fold in the flour and orange rind, then gently mix in the orange juice to make a soft dropping consistency. Grease a 1.2L/2 pint pudding basin and carefully spoon in the mixture. Cover with greaseproof paper and either pleated foil or a fitting lid. Stand in a large saucepan. Pour in boiling water to come half-way up the sides of the basin. Cover, bring to the boil and simmer for 30 minutes, then transfer to a simmering oven for 2¹/₂–3 hours.

Orange Sauce
600ml/1 pint orange juice or 300ml/¹/₂ pint
concentrated orange juice
25–50g/1–2 oz sugar
1 tsp cornflour
1 tbsp cold water

If using ordinary orange juice, boil to reduce to 300ml/¹/₂ pint. Add sugar to taste. Mix together the cornflour and water, and whisk into the hot orange juice. Cook for 3–4 minutes, whisking, until a good sauce is formed.

Serves 6

STEAMED FRUIT PUDDING

This is a suet pastry pudding into which you can put any fruits you have available such as apples, plums, blackcurrants. It is a perfect pudding to prepare in the morning and serve in the evening as the moisture in the fruit means that the pudding needs a lot of cooking.

275g/10 oz plain flour
100g/4 oz castor sugar
1 tsp baking powder
150g/5 oz shredded suet
200ml/7 fl oz milk
450g–900g/1–2 lb prepared chosen fruit
sugar, to taste

Sieve the flour, castor sugar and baking powder into a bowl and stir in the suet. Bind together with enough milk to make pliable dough. Cut off two-thirds and roll into a circle. Use to line a 1.2L/2 pint pudding basin. Fill with fruit and sugar to taste. Roll the remaining pastry to make a lid. Seal well. Cover with greaseproof paper and foil, and stand in a large saucepan. Pour enough boiling water into the pan to come half-way up the sides of the basin. Bring to the boil on the hotplate and simmer for 30 minutes. Transfer to a simmering oven for 5 hours or longer, depending on the fruit.

Serves 6–8

MARMALADE PUDDING

Good for using up leftover home-made marmalade from the previous year after making a new batch in January. This recipe uses a lot of oranges, which are plentiful and juicy then. Serve with the whisky sauce.

5 oranges (some are used in the sauce)
175g/6 oz butter, softened
175g/6 oz castor sugar
3 eggs, beaten
175g/6 oz self-raising flour
6 tbsp marmalade

Sauce
75g/3 oz butter
75g/3 oz castor sugar
3 tbsp whisky
2 tbsp marmalade

Finely grate the rind from one orange. Squeeze the juice from three oranges. Peel the remaining two and cut the flesh into segments.

Cream together the butter and sugar. Add the grated orange rind and beat in the eggs. Fold in the flour, marmalade and 2 tablespoons of orange juice. Spoon 4 tablespoons of marmalade into a 1.2L/2 pint greased pudding basin, and top with the sponge mixture. Cover with greaseproof paper and either foil or a fitting lid. Place in a large saucepan and pour in enough boiling water to come half-way up the sides of the basin. Cover, bring to the boil and simmer for 30 minutes. Transfer to a simmering oven for 2–2½ hours.

To make the sauce, melt together the butter and the sugar over a gentle heat. Cook gently until golden brown. Add the whisky and the remaining orange juice and cook until syrupy. Off the heat, stir in the marmalade and the orange segments. Turn out the pudding and serve with the whisky sauce.

Serves 6-8

PLUM DUFF

....

This pudding was my father's favourite, preferrably served with rice pudding!

225g/8 oz plain flour
2 tsp baking powder
1 tsp mixed spice
75g/3 oz castor sugar
100g/4 oz shredded suet
175g/6 oz raisins
300ml/$\frac{1}{2}$ pint milk

Sieve together the flour, baking powder, spice and sugar. Stir in the suet and raisins. Blend in the milk and place in a buttered 1.2L/2 pint pudding basin. There should be enough room for the pudding to rise. Cover with greaseproof paper and foil or a lid. Stand in a deep saucepan and pour in enough boiling water to come half-way up the sides of the basin. Cover, bring to the boil and simmer for 30 minutes. Transfer to a simmering oven for 3–4 hours.

Serves 6

....

RICH RICE PUDDING

....

This recipe was sent to me by Mrs Peters in Lancashire. It is truly delicious. I find this best to make in a cast-iron dish that will go on the hot plate, into the oven and look good at the table.

60g/2½ oz butter
40g/1 ½ oz caster sugar
90g/3½ oz pudding rice
1.2 Litre/2 pint full cream milk
½ vanilla pod or ½ tsp vanilla essence

Put the butter in the cast-iron dish and place on the hotplate to melt. Stir in the sugar and cook until the mixture becomes toffee-like in consistency, but not brown, Add the rice and stir well until it is sticky and coated. Add the milk and the vanilla pod, if using. (Add vanilla essence later.) Squash the pod to remove the seeds while bringing the mixture gently to the boil. Remove the pod or add essence at this point.

When the milk is boiling, transfer to a simmering oven for 4 hours. This is best served warm, not hot straight from the oven.

Serves 6–8, depending upon appetite!

....

RICE PUDDING

....

This has to be one of the Rayburn-owners easiest puddings. This recipe will only work with full-cream milk! A spoonful of cream will make this special.

75g/3 oz pudding rice
50g/2 oz sugar
1.2L/2 pint milk
25g/1 oz butter

Put the rice in a buttered 1.7L/3 pint ovenproof dish. Sprinkle on the sugar and pour in the milk. Dot with butter.

Stand on the hotplate and allow to come slowly to the boil, stirring once or twice. Then allow a skin to form. Transfer to a simmering oven for 4–5 hours.

Serves 8

....

GOLDEN BREAD PUDDING

....

Use stale croissants or brioche to give a slightly special bread and butter pudding.

4 large croissants, cut in half
50g/2 oz butter
3 eggs
300ml/1/2 pint milk
300ml/1/2 pint single cream
4 tbsp golden syrup

Spread the croissants with the butter and lay in a buttered ovenproof dish. Mix the eggs, milk and cream together and strain over the croissants. Drizzle over the golden syrup. Stand the dish in a roasting tin and pour round boiling water. Put the tin on the second from bottom set of runners of the top oven set to 'Bake' for 30 mins and then transfer to the lower oven or reduce the top oven temperature to 'Simmer' for 1 1/2–2 hours.

Serves 4–6.

....

CHICHESTER PUDDING

....

I started my teaching career in Chichester and have fond memories of that beautiful city. I hope you enjoy the pudding!

6 eggs, separated
75g/3 oz sugar
600ml/1 pint milk
pinch ground cinnamon
175g/6 oz fresh white breadcrumbs

Beat the egg yolks and sugar together in a basin. Warm the milk and cinnamon together in a saucepan and pour over the egg mixture, whisking. Place the breadcrumbs in a bowl and strain the custard on to them. Whisk the egg whites until stiff and gently fold into the custard mixture. Do not over-mix as there should be a marbled effect.

Pour into a 1.2L/2 pint buttered oven–proof dish. Stand in the roasting tin. Pour boiling water round the dish and bake for 20 minutes in the top oven set to 'Bake' and then reduce heat to a simmer for 2 hours until set.

Serves 6

....

HAZELNUT MERINGUES

These meringues are good sandwiched together with cream and fruit or even a little melted chocolate. You can make individual meringues or make two layers to sandwich together for a pudding.

225g/8 oz caster sugar
1 tsp cornflour
4 egg whites
175g/6 oz hazelnuts, toasted and finely chopped

Filling
150ml/1/4 pint double cream, whipped
225g/8 oz raspberries or strawberries, optional
50g/2 oz plain chocolate, melted

Line the cold shelf with baking parchment or Bake-O-Glide. Mix the sugar and cornflour. Whisk the egg whites until stiff but not dry. Continue whisking and add the sugar one teaspoonful at a time. Fold in the hazelnuts.

Spoon two circles of meringue mixture on the prepared cold shelf. Slide into the middle of a simmering oven for 2–4 hours. Leave to cool.

Place one circle of meringue on a serving plate, spread over the whipped cream and scatter over the fruit, if using. Drizzle over some of the melted chocolate. Place the second meringue on top and drizzle over the remaining chocolate.

Serves 6

BROWN SUGAR MERINGUES

The brown sugar gives a rich colour and caramel flavour. If you want to store these, make sure they are dried out well.

100g/4 oz caster sugar
100g/4 oz soft brown sugar
3 egg whites
whipped cream

Weigh the sugars and mix together. Line the cold shelf with baking parchment or Bake-O-Glide. Whisk the egg whites until thick and fluffy, but not dry. As you continue to whisk, add the sugar 1 teaspoonful at a time.

Pipe or spoon individual meringues on to the prepared cold shelf. Slide into the middle of a simmering oven for at least 2–3 hours or even overnight. Store in an airtight container until needed. Sandwich together with whipped cream.

Note: to prevent 'weeping' of the meringues do not whisk in the sugar too quickly. Do not dry out more than one tray at a time.

Makes about 16

DRIED FRUIT COMPÔTE

....

This is such an easy pudding to make. It is delicious served hot or cold. The range of dried fruits available mean that you can ring the changes from something simple like apple rings, prunes and apricots to more exotic combinations with peaches and mangoes.

450g/1 lb assorted dried fruits
grated rind and juice of 1 orange
1 tbsp whisky

Soak the dried fruits for 2–3 hours in cold water. (If the fruits have been in your cupboard sometime they may need longer soaking.)

Place in a flameproof casserole with the soaking water, orange juice and rind, and whisky. The fruits should be just covered by liquid, add more water if necessary. Cover and bring gently to the boil.

Transfer to a simmering oven and allow to cook for 1–2 hours, until the fruits are cooked but not losing their shape. Serve warm or cold.

Serves 6

....

PEARS IN RED WINE

This is a good way to cook under-ripe pears. The cooking time will vary according to the ripeness of the fruit.

300ml/½ pint red wine
225g/8 oz sugar
2 cloves or 1 cinnamon stick
1 kg/2 lb 4 oz pears, peeled, halved and cored
flaked almonds, to decorate

Pour the wine into a saucepan, add the sugar and the cloves or cinnamon. Dissolve the sugar over gentle heat, bring to the boil and then add the prepared pears. Cover and transfer to a simmering oven for 1½–2 hours. Sprinkle with almonds and serve warm with cream.

Serves 6–8.

BAKED APPLES

An autumn favourite. Experiment with different fillings.

cooking apples, one per person
sugar
butter
golden syrup

Core the apples and make a horizontal slit in the skin round the middle. Stand in an ovenproof dish. Put a little sugar into each apple. Dot each apple with butter and drizzle over a little golden syrup. Put 1–2 tablespoons water in the bottom of the dish. Put the shelf on the bottom set of runners of the top oven set to 'Bake' and put in the apples for 30–40 minutes.

CRÈME BRULÉE

This is a rich, creamy dessert best made the day before it is needed because it does require chilling. Six ramekin dishes will fit into the roasting tin.

500ml/1 pint double cream
1 vanilla pod or 1 tsp vanilla essence
4 egg yolks
50g/2 oz caster sugar

Pour the cream into a saucepan and add the vanilla pod (add vanilla essence later). Stand on the hotplate to warm through. Place the egg yolks into a basin with the sugar and whisk until thick and fluffy. Remove the vanilla pod from the cream and pour the cream onto the egg mixture, whisking. If using vanilla essence, whisk this in at this point. Strain into a jug.

Stand six ramekins in the small roasting tin and pour the custard into each one. Pour hot water into the roasting tin to come half-way up the sides of the ramekins. Slide into a simmering oven and cook for 2–3 hours until set. The mixture will still be slightly wobbly even when cooked. Cool overnight.

Caramel Topping

Unless you have a very hot domestic grill, it is difficult to get a successful brulée topping. Some people use a blow torch! I make caramel and pour over. Place 100g/4 oz granulated sugar in a saucepan and stand over a low heat. Warm to dissolve the sugar, but try not to stir. When the sugar has melted keep an eye on the pan as the sugar burns easily. Heat the pan until the sugar turns a pale caramel colour and then drizzle the caramel over the chilled custards. Serve. Do not stand for too long or the caramel will soften.

Serves 6

'WICKED' WALNUT PUDDING

This is possibly the richest and most calorific pudding I make! The name comes from my children, 'wicked' meaning exceptionally good!

150g/5 oz butter
175g/6 oz soft brown sugar
300ml/½ pint double cream
100g/4 oz dates, chopped
½ tsp bicarbonate soda
1 egg
100g/4 oz self-raising flour
50g/2 oz walnuts, chopped

In a small saucepan warm together 75g/3 oz of the butter and 100g/4 oz of the sugar. Stir in the cream. Bring to the boil and bubble fast for a few minutes to make a fudge sauce. Put the dates in a basin and cover with 150ml/¼ pint of boiling water and the bicarbonate of soda. Leave to stand for 10 minutes to soften the dates.

Cream together the remaining 50g/2 oz butter and 50g/2 oz sugar. Beat in the egg and the date mixture. Fold in the flour and the walnuts. Do not worry if the mixture looks curdled at this stage!

Pour 2–3 tablespoons of the fudge sauce into the base of a greased 1.2L/2 pint pudding basin. Spoon in the pudding mixture. Cover with greaseproof paper and foil or a lid. Stand the basin in a deep saucepan and pour in enough boiling water to come half-way up the sides of the basin. Cover and bring the water to the boil. Simmer for 30 minutes, then transfer to a simmering oven for 2–3 hours. Turn out and serve with the remaining fudge sauce.

Serves 6

CHUTNEYS

CHUTNEYS

The Rayburn is the perfect cooker for making chutney. By using a low simmering oven for the long slow cooking, the vinegar smell will disappear up the chimney and not invade the house. There is also no need to constantly watch the pot for burning. Long, slow cooking of chutney improves the flavour.

Again, a good-sized preserving pan is useful, and as the chutney is not boiled rapidly the pan can be about two-thirds full. Jar lids need to be coated to prevent corrosion by the vinegar. Warm in the simmering oven before filling. Brown and white sugar can be used. Dark brown sugar will give a darker chutney and a rich flavour. Similarly dark malt vinegar will colour the chutney, while for a lighter pickle you can use white wine vinegar.

I know it is tempting to try the chutney as soon as it is made, but it really needs 4–6 weeks for the flavours to develop and the strong vinegar flavour to mellow. Use jars that are scrupulously clean and lids that are acid-resistant.

CRANBERRY CHUTNEY

Most people associate cranberries with Christmas, and this chutney makes a very welcome Christmas gift. Frozen cranberries are available all year round, so make this at any time to go with poultry.

700g/1 lb 8 oz cranberries
300ml/$\frac{1}{2}$ pint wine vinegar
225g/8 oz sultanas
grated rind and segments from 3 oranges
100g/4 oz sugar
15g/$\frac{1}{2}$ oz salt
2 tsp ground cinnamon
2 tsp ground allspice

Wash and pick over the cranberries. Place in a preserving pan or large saucepan with the remaining ingredients. Stand on the hotplate and heat gently to dissolve the sugar. Stir well, cover and bring to the boil. Remove the lid and transfer to a simmering oven and cook for 1–1$\frac{1}{2}$ hours until thick. Pour into jars, cover and label.

Makes about 1kg/2 lb 4 oz

APRICOT CHUTNEY

This can be made at any time of year if your supplies are running low. This is particularly good with cold pork and pork pies.

450g/1 lb dried apricots, chopped
450g/1 lb sultanas
4 large onions, chopped
12 fresh red chillies, seeded and chopped
900ml/1½ pints malt vinegar
450g/1 lb brown sugar
25g/1 oz salt

Use either a mincer or a processor for this. Mince the apricots, sultanas, onions and chillies together. Do not over-process. Place in a preserving pan with the vinegar, brown sugar and salt. Bring to the boil, transfer to a simmering oven and cook for 2–2½ hours until thick. Pour into jars, seal and label.

Makes about 1.8kg/4 lb

PLUM CHUTNEY

....

Make this when plums are plentiful or substitute rhubarb or damsons for the plums. Lovely with cold meat.

450g/1 lb onions, chopped
450g/1 lb cooking apples, peeled and cored
2kgs/4 lb 8 oz plums, halved and stoned
225g/8 oz sultanas
600ml/1 pint vinegar
600g/1 lb 8oz soft brown sugar
25g/1 oz salt
4 cloves
1 piece dried root ginger, bruised
1 tsp mustard seeds
2 black peppercorns

Place the onions and apples in a large preserving pan or saucepan. Add the plums, sultanas, vinegar, sugar and salt. Put the cloves, ginger, mustard seeds and peppercorns in a muslin bag and bury this in the mixture. Cover, place the pan on the hotplate and bring slowly to the boil, stirring occasionally. When boiling well, remove the lid and place in a simmering oven for about 2 hours until the mixture is thick and jam-like. Pour into jars, seal and label.

Makes about 2.25kg/5 lb

....

BANANA AND DATE CHUTNEY

I make this after Christmas to use up left-over dates and bananas. The chutney will be dark and rich.

1kg/2 lb 4 oz bananas, peeled and sliced
500g stoned dates, chopped
1kg/2 lb 4 oz cooking apples, peeled, cored and chopped
grated rind and juice of 2 oranges
2 tsp mixed spice
2 tsp ground ginger
2 tsp curry powder
2 tsp salt
600ml/1 pint malt vinegar
450g/1 lb sugar

Place all the ingredients in a large saucepan or preserving pan and mix well. Stand on the hotplate and slowly bring to the boil, stirring occasionally. Transfer to a simmering oven for 1½–2 hours, until thick.

Makes about 3kg/6 lb 8oz

DRIED FRUIT CHUTNEY

A store-cupboard chutney. Chop the fruits to whatever consistency you like. Allow time for the fruits to soak overnight.

225g/8 oz dried apricots, chopped
225g/8 oz dried peaches, chopped
600ml/1 pint wine vinegar
450g/1 lb cooking apples, peeled, cored and chopped
225g/8 oz raisins
100g/4 oz dates, chopped
2 onions, chopped
2 cloves garlic, crushed
1/2 tsp salt
1/2 tsp ground coriander
1/2 tsp ground cloves
1 tsp dry mustard powder
pinch cayenne pepper
675g/1 lb 8 oz soft brown sugar

Place the apricots and peaches in a bowl with the vinegar. Leave to stand overnight. Transfer the mixture to a preserving pan and bring to the boil. Add the apples, raisins, dates, and onions. Stir well. Add the remaining ingredients, bring to the boil and transfer to a simmering oven for 1 1/2–2 hours until the mixture is thick. Pour into jars, cover and label.

Makes about 2.25kg/5 lb

GREEN TOMATO CHUTNEY

Green tomato chutney is a good enough reason to grow your own tomatoes – where else do you get green tomatoes for this lovely chutney?

450g/1 lb onions, chopped
2.25kg/5 lb green tomatoes, chopped
½ tsp salt
15g/½ oz pickling spice, tied in a muslin bag
600ml/1 pint malt vinegar
450g/1 lb sugar

Put the onions in a large saucepan or preserving pan with a little water and stand on the hotplate to cook until softening. Add the tomatoes, salt and pickling spice and half the vinegar. Bring to the boil and place in the simmering oven for about 1½-2 hours until thick. Remove the pickling spice. Now stir in the sugar and the remaining vinegar. Dissolve the sugar over medium heat and when bubbling return to a simmering oven for another hour, until the mixture is like thick jam. Pour into jars, seal and label.

Makes about 2.25kg/5lb

TOMATO SAUCE

I like this preserved tomato sauce instead of tomato ketchup. If you like a smooth sauce, purée the mixture after cooking. This is a sauce, not a thick chutney.

18 large tomatoes, peeled and chopped
6 large onions, chopped
600ml/1 pint vinegar
100g/4 oz sugar
2 scant tbsp salt

Place all the ingredients in a saucepan or preserving pan. Stand on the simmering plate and heat to dissolve the sugar. Bring to the boil and transfer to a simmering oven for about 2 hours. Bottle, seal and label.

INDEX

SOUPS AND STARTERS

MAIN COURSES

ACCOMPANIMENTS

PUDDINGS

CHUTNEYS

ACKNOWLEDGEMENTS

....

I have to thank all the Rayburn customers in Bath, Cardiff, Neath and Dorchester who kindly asked me for another book. They have been a tremendous encouragement. As usual, Jon Croft of Absolute Press, who seems to have faith in me, and Bron Douglas, my editor, who keeps me going through thick and thin, have been a great help.

A good friend, Marian Jones and her family have willingly eaten a variety of recipe tests and usually come back with complimentary comments!

My family bear the brunt of any new book being written. Hanna can now have her stir-fries and quick pastas that she was longing for in the middle of testing so many casseroles. Dominic and Hugo have suffered winter soups and steamed puddings as temperatures reached 28°C at the beginning of their much-needed summer holiday. My biggest thanks must be to Geoff, my husband, who encourages me all the way, even when I can't get on with the computer or a recipe fails.

Louise Walker
July, 1997

COOK'S NOTES

COOK'S NOTES

AGA AND RAYBURN TITLES
BY LOUISE WALKER

The Traditional Aga Cookery Book (£9.99)
The Traditional Aga Party Book (£9.99)
The Traditional Aga Book of Slow Cooking (£9.99)

The Traditional Aga Box Set (£29.50)
(comprising all three of the above titles)

The Traditional Aga Book of Vegetarian Cooking (£9.99)
The Traditional Aga Four Seasons Cookery Book (£9.99)

Forthcoming
The Traditional Aga Book of Breads and Cakes (£9.99)
The Traditional Aga Box Set 2 (£29.50)
(comprising all three of the above titles)

The Classic Rayburn Cookery Book (£9.99)
The Classic Rayburn Book of Slow Cooking (£9.99)

The Classic Rayburn Box Set (£19.50)
(comprising both of the above titles)

Aga Cakes Magnet-Book (£2.99)
Aga Pickles Magnet-Book (£2.99)
Aga Pies Magnet-Book (£2.99)
Aga Soups Magnet-Book (£2.99)

All titles are available to order from Absolute Press.

Send cheques, made payable to Absolute Press,
or VISA/Mastercard details to Absolute Press,
Scarborough House, 29 James Street West, Bath BA1 2BT.
Phone 01225 316 013 for any further details.

THE CLASSIC
RAYBURN
COOKERY BOOK

First published in 1996 by Absolute Press, Scarborough House,
29 James Street West, Bath, BA1 2BT. Tel: 01225 316013 Fax: 01225 445836
email sales@absolutepress.co.uk

Reprinted March 1997
Reprinted June 1998
Reprinted April 2000
Reprinted July 2002
Reprinted December 2003

© Louise Walker 1996

The rights of Louise Walker to be identified as author of this work have been
asserted by her in accordance with the Copyright Designs and Patents Act 1988.

ISBN 1 899791 45 0

Cover and text Design by Ian Middleton
Cover and text illustrations by Caroline Nisbett

Printed by Butler & Tanner Ltd, Frome and London
Covers printed by Lawrence-Allen Ltd, Weston-Super-Mare

No part of this publication may be reproduced, stored in a retrieval system or
transmitted in any form or by any means electronic, mechanical, photocopying,
recording or otherwise without the prior permission of Absolute Press.

THE CLASSIC
RAYBURN
COOKERY BOOK

LOUISE WALKER

ABSOLUTE PRESS

CONTENTS

....

G E N E R A L
I N T R O D U C T I O N

A BRIEF NOTE ABOUT USING THIS RAYBURN BOOK

Rayburns come in a variety of models. Before you start cooking with your particular Rayburn read the instruction manual that comes with it. Some models have a cast-iron lower oven which can be used for cooking; this is usually at half the temperature that the top oven is set at. Those models that do not have this facility may use the lower oven for keeping food warm, warming plates etc. The cooking instructions in this book have been given for all types of Rayburn using the top oven only. However, if your Rayburn has the cast-iron lower oven try cooking at low temperatures in the lower oven when the top oven is set to Roast 230C/450F. For example, when roasting meat in the top oven, potatoes and root vegetables will cook very well in the lower oven, perhaps alongside a steamed pudding.

The position of the hottest spot on the plate varies from model to model. However, the continuous plate means that pans can be slid along the plate according to the amount of heat needed. If the hotplate is too hot or you need to use a lot of saucepans it is easy to arrange the pans half on and half off the hotplate.

CONVERSION CHART

This is the metric/imperial conversion chart that I have used. Do keep to either metric or imperial measures throughout the whole recipe; mixing the two can lead to all kinds of problems. Eggs used in testing have been size 3. Tablespoon and teaspoon measures have been flat unless otherwise stated.

Flour is always plain unless stated.

Conversion Table

1 oz	25g
2 oz	50g
3 oz	75g
4 oz	100g
5 oz	150g
6 oz	175g
7 oz	200g
8 oz	225g
9 oz	250g
10 oz	275g
11 oz	300g
12 oz	350g
13 oz	375g
14 oz	400g
15 oz	425g
16 oz (1 lb)	450g
2lbs	1kg
1 tsp	5ml
1 tbsp	15ml
¼ pint	150ml
½ pint	300ml
¾ pint	450ml
1 pint	600ml
2 pints	1 litre
8 inch tin	20cm tin

GENERAL INTRODUCTION

This book is intended as a useful handbook for Rayburn owners. It cannot be a definitive recipe book, but I have tried to cover all the basic topics that crop up when teaching new and experienced Rayburn owners how to use their Rayburn to full effect. I hope it will be a constant reference point and a basis for using other new and well tried recipes with confidence.

I know from the demonstrating and workshop sessions I run, that there are two types of Rayburn owner: Those who choose a Rayburn to put into their home and those who inherit a Rayburn when they move house. The former have either been brought up with a Rayburn, or they have had the opportunity to observe the multitude of benefits bestowed by the presence of a Rayburn. The latter are often terrified by the great monster in the kitchen, but after only a few months, the fear has gone and they are quite converted.

We all love the constant warmth when the Rayburn is on. This is why so many owners leave their Rayburn to idle at a low heat, thus creating that heart to the kitchen.

I have yet to find a Rayburn owner, new or old, who would change to another cooker, let alone give up all those other "conveniences". The most popular selling Rayburns at the moment are gas-fired. However, not so long ago solid fuel was the popular fuel for Rayburns and some people still think that Rayburns can only be properly run on solid fuel. In fact many other fuels can be used: electricity, liquid propane, gas and oil.

The solid fuel Rayburns are the most complicated to run and, if yours is one of those, your own experience will tell you how to fuel it for the particular cooking task in hand. Fortunately this experience does not take long to acquire. As with all Rayburns, keep the lids down as much as possible; some people open the vent door to give an extra boost of heat during cooking. Rayburns converted from solid fuel to oil or gas often have "personality" differences. For example, the ovens may prove difficult to regulate for various recipes. However, "personality" differences are fairly typical of all Rayburns, as they are made individually and are sited and fuelled differently.

Like all new kitchen appliances, it takes time to get to know your Rayburn; perhaps this is the secret of the great Rayburn-owners' loyalty – it becomes a personality in the kitchen. However, all this does mean that writing recipes for a Rayburn can in no way be regarded as an "exact science". Almost everything should be treated as guidelines. I hope that the recipes in this book will give you ideas on the efficient use of your Rayburn and on its range of capabilities. You can then go on to experiment confidently with other recipes.

LOOKING AFTER YOUR
RAYBURN

If you are doing a lot of cooking or entertaining, for example, at Christmas, turn up the Rayburn a little more than usual. If you have an automatic timer, you may need to over-ride the preset controls for that day or your Christmas dinner may be later than you expected!

If you are used to the chore of cleaning a gas or electric cooker, you will love the simplicity of keeping the Rayburn clean. Mine gets a thorough clean just once a year, when it is switched off for servicing; mine is gas-fired, an oil-fired one needs 6-monthly servicing. The night before servicing I switch off the Rayburn completely. After the breakfast is cleared away I set to on the cleaning and try to do as much as possible before the engineer arrives. Remove everything possible; the oven shelves and the doors which simply lift off. Brush out all the carbon deposits from the ovens. Anything still sticky on the floor of the oven can be removed with a wooden spatula, and the remains left to carbonise.

Clean the lids of the boiling plate, simmering plate and round the inside of the oven door frames with a warm soapy cloth and a paste cleaner such as Astonish. **Never** be tempted to use a wire wool pad or a tough abrasive. Some elbow grease may be needed but you will be surprised how much dirt will come off. Rinse off with a clean cloth and buff up. Clean the oven shelves in a sink of soapy water and more Astonish if needed. Replace. Wipe round the doors and clean the inside of the top and lower oven doors if necessary. The other doors will probably not get dirty. If you are concerned about the state of

the seals remember to get the engineer to check them. Return all the bits and pieces to their places and give the whole Rayburn a wipe down and buff up. I know some people who polish their Rayburns occasionally! Other than the annual clean try to wipe up any spills as they occur and wipe off any other crumbs, dust and so on daily. I find a lot of dust on my Rayburn, partly due to all the laundry put to dry or air above it.

POTS, PANS AND ACCESSORIES

Many people worry about their saucepans when they have a new Rayburn. New pans purchased with a Rayburn will last a lifetime if they are looked after, because there is no warping of the bases due to the even heat area. However, it isn't always necessary to rush out and buy pans. Think carefully about what you need and buy one at a time.

If you have existing pans there are two ways of testing their suitability for the Rayburn. Turn the pan upside down and put a ruler or something with a straight edge across the base. If daylight shows through the pan will not work efficiently. Alternatively half fill the pan with water and put on the boiling plate to boil. If only a poor contact is being made the water will not boil. Beware – even toast crumbs on the plate can have the same effect. A good, heavy-based pan is best. The size, shape and metal varies so choose according to your personal needs and preferences. Pans that go on the hot plates and in the oven are very useful. The Rayburn showroom will have a good range to show you.

A kettle is useful, especially if you leave your Rayburn on all the time and always have heat ready to boil water, but the shape and style are your own personal preference. Choose a heavy base and ask if you can do a water pouring test in the showroom or shop so that you know that the kettle suits you.

The Rayburn tin is useful because it fits the runners of the oven and can be used as an extra shelf the roasting rack for the tin is handy to use when roasting fatty meat, or for grilling bacon, sausages and chops.

You will use oven-proof dishes quite a lot because so much cooking is done in the ovens. I find pans and casseroles that can be used on the top plates and in the oven especially useful but beware, wooden or plastic "handles" as those on the Agaluxe range cannot be used in the top oven when it is above simmering heat

and in time wooden handles will dry out and come apart. Cast iron pans and dishes are useful for their multi-purpose use but they can be heavy to lift!

COOKING WITH THE RAYBURN

The Rayburn uses a certain amount of stored heat, and the ovens cook really well when they are evenly heated, so the aim is to cook with as little heat loss as possible. As soon as the hot plate lids are raised, heat will be lost, so use the ovens as much as possible. Of course, that way all the smells and condensation go up the chimney.

Frying and steaming and grilling can be done in the oven, while toast is done by placing the bread directly on the simmering end of the hot plate.

The hot plate is one continuous piece across the top of the cooker but is varied in heat. Each model Rayburn has its own "hot spot". The hottest area is used for boiling the kettle, fast boiling green vegetables and stir-frying. The cooler areas are used to simmer gently, making sauces, doing toast on and cooking drop scones and Welsh cakes. The hot plate is slightly raised above the enamelled top, as this helps prevent scratching when pans are pulled slightly off the heat if the contents are cooking too fast. You can melt chocolate, butter and syrups and warm milk simply by standing the food in a bowl on top of the Rayburn. To maintain heat, the heavy insulated lids are kept down when the hot plate is not in use. The shiny lids are slightly domed. Do not be tempted to put the kettle or other pots and pans on the lid without using a protective pad: once scratched always scratched. Always remember – as soon as cooking is finished put the lids down so that heat is restored.

The ovens, which look so small from the outside, are very spacious inside. Rayburn roasting tins are designed to fit exactly so they will slide on the runners without the use of the oven shelf. Rayburns are now supplied with a roasting tin with a rack to fit. The rack makes a useful cooling rack when you are doing a lot of baking. Two oven shelves with useful anti-tilt devices are also supplied. If you have the opportunity, try sliding the shelves in and out of the oven before the Rayburn is fired up. They are easy to use once you have the knack, but difficult to manage when hot if you have not tried it before. I know one couple who spent a whole day trying to get their shelves out! The mysterious cold plain shelf is also supplied. This also fits the runners and can be

used as an oven shelf or a baking tray. However, it should be kept out of the oven, somewhere cool, so that it can be used to diffuse the heat when the oven is hot and some food needs to be cooked at a cooler temperature. I met one lady, a Rayburn owner for 30 years, who did not know what the cold plain shelf was really for. No wonder she thought my demonstration was a revelation! More details on how to use this shelf will be found in the recipes, especially those for cake making.

TIPS AND USES FOR THE RAYBURN

One of the best tips I can give when buying a Rayburn is "buy a timer you can carry around with you"! There are no smells from a Rayburn, so it is easy to forget. I think all Rayburn owners have opened the oven and thought "what WAS that lump of charcoal?" Those yellow sticky note pads are useful – reminders on the breakfast table to "remember porridge" or "remember stock/Christmas cakes/puddings etc". I have been known to put a reminder "remember casserole" on my pillow so that I remove it before going to bed!

Dry baking tins and awkwardly shaped cooking utensils on top of the Rayburn – there are no excuses for rusty tins.

Pastry cases for quiches do not need to be "baked blind". Simply cook them directly on the floor of the roasting oven for a crisp base. It is safe to use porcelain, glass and metal flan dishes.

Stand mugs of tea or coffee on top of the Rayburn to keep warm when the telephone rings.

To defrost cakes or bread, stand them on top of the simmering plate lid or place in the simmering oven.

Dry the washing on top of the simmering plate lid – the boiling plate is too hot. Spin the items to be dried, smooth out any creases and lay on the lid: no ironing needed! Hang towels or sheets over the chrome rail – just take care not to cover the air vents on the control box door.

If your kitchen ceiling is high enough a kitchen maid above the Rayburn is useful for drying washing. Hang flowers to dry on the ends so that it does

not look too utilitarian.

Rugby boots washed of all their mud, and washed trainers, can be hung by their laces on the chrome rail and dried.
Shoes wet from winter rain should be stuffed full with newspaper and dried in front of the Rayburn – the gentle heat will not spoil the leather.

When the snow comes the Rayburn heat is busy not just producing hot food but drying snowy gloves and socks, as well as warming coats and hats and boots.

Finally, a word about oven gloves. Go for the long Rayburn gauntlets: no more burnt arms reaching to the back of the oven to get that elusive dish or potato.

20 QUESTIONS ANSWERED

1. DO I REALLY NEED ANOTHER COOKER FOR BAKING CAKES AND BISCUITS?
No. With the Rayburn, biscuits and cakes can easily be baked without burning by either having the oven on the "Bake" setting or if the temperature is higher, e.g. "Roast" use the cold plain shelf.

2. DO I NEED TO BUY A WHOLE SET OF PANS TO GO WITH MY NEW RAYBURN?
Take your time about choosing pans. It is important that they have a ground base for making good contact with the boiling and simmering plates. Each family has different needs for shapes, sizes of pans, so look at the range available for use with a Rayburn before choosing. See the Introduction Section on Pots and Pans for more detail.

3. THERE IS NO GRILL ON THE RAYBURN, HOW WILL I GRILL CHOPS AND BROWN FOOD? DO I HAVE TO RETURN TO FRYING?
A grill isn't needed on the Rayburn because food put in the highest position of the roasting oven will brown in the same way as with a grill. Either place the oven shelf on the right runner possible or use the roasting tin hung on the top set of runners. This tin is just like a grill pan if the rack is fitted inside. Chops and sausages cook in just the same way as with a grill without the mess and a more moist result!

Frying can be done on the floor of the top oven should you wish to cook that way. Cast-iron pans work very well on the floor of the top oven as well as the hot plates.

4. ALL MY FRIENDS TELL ME THAT IT IS EASY TO RUN OUT OF HEAT. WILL I MANAGE TO COOK A MEAL FOR A CROWD?
Yes, easily. Heat is lost as soon as the lids are lifted and so to prevent heat loss and filling the kitchen with steam and smells cook as much as possible in the oven.

Virtually everything can be cooking in the oven, read the book and find out!

5. **HOW CAN I COOK MASSES OF VEGETABLES TO GO WITH THE SUNDAY ROAST WITHOUT THE TEMPERATURE DROPPING?**

Turn the Rayburn up to a high heat if you are cooking a large meal so there is plenty of heat in both ovens. All root vegetables can be cooked in the oven, thus saving heat. Place the vegetables in a saucepan with salt to taste and half covered with water. Stand on the boiling plate, cover with a lid and bring to the boil. Boil for 1-2 minutes. If time is short leave the water in the pan and transfer directly to the simmering oven. Alternatively, if preparing well in advance, drain the water off and transfer, in the hot saucepan, to the lower oven.

Green vegetables are best cooked quickly, so plunge into fast boiling, salted water for the minimum cooking time to give crisp, bright vegetables – alternatively steam the vegetables.

6. **CAN I STILL USE MY WOK, STIR-FRYING IS SUCH A PART OF MY COOKING THESE DAYS?**

Woks really rely on a good heat source up the side of the pan so that food can be cooked all over the surface of the Wok. This heating is not satisfactory on the Rayburn boiling plate, however I find a large, deep frying pan almost the size of the hot plate is perfect for stir-frying, but get the pan *really* hot first. Put on the heat completely empty for 4-5 minutes before starting to cook.

7. **MUST I USE RAYBURN RECIPES ONLY OR CAN I ADAPT MY FAVOURITES? I DON'T FEEL VERY CONFIDENT.**

Any recipe can be used, but confidence is the key to successful use of the Rayburn. Like any new piece of kitchen equipment take time to read the recipe/instruction books, be prepared for some mistakes and experiment. The recipes in the book have been chosen to illustrate the basic methods needed when using the Rayburn. As a guideline: the hottest part of the plate is for boiling, stir-frying and rapid cooking; the cooler parts are for simmering, sautéing, making sauces, heating milk; the roasting oven is very hot, and the nearer the top the hotter the oven; the top oven is a more moderate heat; the lower oven is cooler and can be used for plate warming and holding warm foods, except when the top oven is on "Roast". The lower oven can then be used to cook soups, stews, casseroles and so on.

8. SHOULD I TURN THE RAYBURN OFF WHEN I GO AWAY FOR THE WEEKEND?

Not necessarily. For a weekend, the Rayburn is usually happy left on its usual setting, particularly if it is on an automatic timer. For longer periods, turn the Rayburn off.

9. WHY DOES THE TEMPERATURE DROP SO MUCH WHEN I OPEN THE OVEN DOOR?

The oven temperature dial is positioned on the door, so when the door is opened the oven temperature appears to drop. To get a more accurate reading of the temperature in the centre of the oven, close the door and check again after a few minutes.

10. IS IT NECESSARY TO HAVE MY RAYBURN SERVICED REGULARLY?

Yes. For efficient safe running have the Rayburn serviced annually – except oil Rayburns which should be serviced every six months. When the Rayburn is turned off it is a good time to give the Rayburn a good clean. This is the time to bring out the old electric kettle and toaster!

11. MERINGUES MADE IN THE RAYBURN HAVE A WONDERFUL REPUTATION, BUT MINE ARE STICKY AND WET. WHAT AM I DOING WRONG?

Meringues can be tricky and advice difficult. Firstly, when making the meringues the sugar must be whisked in slowly, I only whisk in 1 teaspoonful at a time. Then spoon onto a plain shelf lined with rice paper, silicone paper or Bake-o-Guide.

Slide the tray on the bottom set of runners of the top oven when it is on a low "Simmer" or in the bottom oven if the top oven is on "Roast". Timing is difficult because ovens vary. I cook my meringues for about 4 hours; if they are not as dry as I like I leave them in but with the oven door slightly open. The meringues will dry out but not colour. I have actually forgotten one batch and left them in for over 48 hours – to no harm.

12. I HAVE A RAYBURN CONVERTED FROM SOLID FUEL TO OIL. I FIND THE ROASTING OVEN VERY HOT, EVEN WHEN TURNED LOW. HOW CAN I REGULATE FOR COOKING?

Knowing that your Rayburn is 'hot' compared with other Rayburns you will need to allow shorter cooking time for roasts etc., use a lower shelf, because the top of the oven is always hottest. Use the cold shelf not just for cake and biscuit making, but to cut down heat for other foods.

13. WHEN I COOK FISH FOR A MAIN COURSE CAN I STILL COOK THE PUDDING AT THE SAME TIME OR WILL THE FISH TAINT THE PUDDING?
Because the Rayburn has a proper flue and the air is not being circulated in the oven there will be no overlap of flavours.

14. IF I CAN'T SMELL FOOD COOKING IN THE OVENS, HOW DO I STOP FOOD BURNING?
Equip yourself with a timer, preferably one that is either very loud so you can leave the kitchen, or one to carry round. I have seen a light fixed over Rayburns that are switched on when food goes in the oven. I also use little sticky Post-it labels which I put on the breakfast table to remind of porridge.

15. HOW DO I CLEAN THE RAYBURN WHEN IT IS HOT ALL THE TIME?
As the Rayburn is hot a lot of the time, food spills and splashes will carbonise on the hot plates and in the oven and can be brushed off with a wire brush. Wipe over the vitreous enamel as soon as spills occur, this stops any acid damage to the enamel. The enamelled surface can be cleaned safely with Astonish paste on a damp cloth, then rinsed and buffed up.

16. CAN I DRY MY WASHING ON MY RAYBURN?
Yes. Two points to be careful about. Do not cover any air vents in doors, so that burning of the fuel can continue properly balanced and don't put laundry on the hottest lid as it is hot enough to scorch. Hang laundry on a clothes-horse on a kitchen maid overnight or when you are out. Fold sheets etc. and put on the simmering plate lid to dry or air. They will iron themselves. Don't forget baking tins as well – they can be put to dry so won't rust during storage.

17. THE OVENS SEEM VERY SMALL, I DON'T GET EVERYTHING IN I NEED.
The difference with the Rayburn oven and conventional gas or electric ovens is that the whole space can be used as there are no hot elements or burners. So put tins, dishes etc. right to the back and the sides, and of course the

floor can be used, for example cooking pastry to get a crisp base, cooking 'fried' fish or eggs. The ovens are deep, but remember the shelves can easily be pulled forward to get at things or the Rayburn gauntlets can be used.

18. **I LIKE TO MAKE BREAD. WHERE SHOULD I STAND THE DOUGH TO RISE?**

The Rayburn is perfect for bread-making. The warm, even heat is always to hand for rising. Here are a few tips. Warm the flour at the back of the Rayburn. When the dough is made put it to rise on top or near the Rayburn. If you stand the bowl or baking sheet on the Rayburn remember to use a folded tea-towel or trivet. This not only protects the surface from scratching but stops the dough getting too hot and 'cooking'. Before baking make sure the oven is well up to temperature as bread needs to be baked in a hot oven.

19. **MY FAMILY COME IN AT ALL DIFFERENT TIMES FOR MEALS. CAN I KEEP FOOD HOT ON THE RAYBURN OR SHOULD I JUST RE-HEAT IN MY MICRO-WAVE.**

Food will keep hot and moist in the low temperature lower oven for about an hour without spoiling. Drain rice and vegetables and put in serving dishes, cover and keep warm ready to serve. Sauces keep hot very well if made in advance also.

20. **WHY CAN MY FRIEND COOK CASSEROLES AND SO ON IN HER LOWER OVEN AND I CAN ONLY USE MINE FOR KEEPING FOOD HOT?**

Some models of Rayburn have cast iron lower ovens which can be used for cooking when the top oven is over 200C/400F or on "Roast". On other models the lower oven is only designed to be used as a warming oven.

BASIC RAYBURN TECHNIQUES

FISH

Cooking fish in the Rayburn is so easy and cuts out fishy smells! The variety of fish available is increasing all the time, so experiment with different fish and different cooking methods. I have given approximate cooking times, but this will depend upon the size and thickness of the fish. Try not to overcook as this gives dry, stringy, tasteless fish. Have the oven setting on the hotter end of "Bake" (180C/350F).

POACHING FISH
Place the fish in the roasting tin, cover with water, wine or milk, salt, pepper and a bayleaf. Cover loosely with foil and hang the tin on the third set of runners from the top for 15-20 minutes.

POACHING WHOLE LARGE FISH e.g. SALMON
Clean the fish. Sprinkle with salt if desired, and wrap in buttered foil. Lift the parcel into the roasting tin, pour boiling water into the tin to come half-way up the fish. Hang on the second set of runners from the top of the top oven. Cook for 10 minutes per lb (450g), turning the fish half-way through cooking. Remove from the oven and allow to cool. Serve warm or remove the skin when cold.

FRIED FISH
Wash and dry the fish. If required, coat it with seasoned flour, batter, oatmeal or egg and fresh breadcrumbs. Put enough cooking oil into the roasting tin to coat the base. Put the tin on the floor of the top oven and heat until hazing. Add the fish and continue to cook on the floor of the oven. Turn the fish half-way through the cooking time.

GRILLED FISH
Lay fish cutlets in a roasting tin, brush with oil and seasoning. Hang the tin on the highest set of runners and "grill", turning over half-way through the cooking time. It sometimes rings the changes to marinade the fish for half an hour and grill with the grill rack in the roasting tin, basting or brushing with a little more marinade part way through cooking. This will give a more "charred" appearance and taste.

ROASTING MEAT

Meat roasted in the Rayburn will be moist and flavoursome. Only a smearing of extra fat is needed to start the cooking. Season as you prefer – salt, pepper, fresh herbs etc. If the meat is stuffed do this and then weigh to calculate cooking times. There are two methods of roasting using the Rayburn. The Quick Roasting Method is the more traditional method, used for more tender cuts of meat. The Slow Roasting Method is best for less fine cuts of meat.

QUICK ROASTING METHOD

Put the oven temperature to "Roast", 200C/400F. Season the meat and put in the Rayburn roasting tin. Stand on the grill rack if you like. Hang the tin on the bottom set of runners of the top oven for the calculated time. Baste with hot fat periodically. The shape of the joint will also affect the cooking time – a long narrow joint will not take so long as a short, fat joint. When the meat is cooked, allow the joint to rest in the lower oven for 15 minutes before carving. This is useful time to make gravy and cook last minute green vegetables.

SLOW COOKING METHOD

Season and prepare the meat as above. Put the roasting tin into the top oven on the bottom set of runners for 30 minutes or until the meat is browning and getting hot. Then reduce the oven temperature to "Bake" (150C/300F), and cook for twice the time calculated for the normal roasting method.

TIMES FOR ROASTING:

Roast Beef:	
rare	10 minutes per lb/450g plus 10 minutes
medium	15 minutes per lb/450g plus 15 minutes
well done	20 minutes per lb/450g plus 20 minutes
Fillet	10 minutes per lb/450g plus 10 minutes

Roast Pork:	30 minutes per lb/450g plus 30 minutes

Lamb:	
pink	15 minutes per lb/450g plus 15 minutes
medium	20 minutes per lb/450g plus 20 minutes

Veal:	20 minutes per lb/450g plus 20 minutes

ROASTING POULTRY AND GAME

....

Roast poultry and game from the Rayburn will produce crisp skin on the outside of moist tender flesh. Most poultry is cooked in the roasting oven by the normal method, but a large turkey can be cooked all night with the oven set at "Simmer" (150C/300F), useful when cooking for a crowd or to take the rush and bustle from Christmas morning. Nowadays it is not considered safe to stuff poultry before roasting, though the neck end of turkey can still be filled if not the cavity. Always allow extra cooking time for this stuffing.

Smear the bird with a little butter. Put bacon rashers over the breast if liked. Stand on the trivet in the roasting tin. Put lemon or herbs in the body cavity if liked. Cover with a little foil – not tightly or this will slow the cooking time. Hang the tin on the lowest set of runners for the following times. Remove the foil for the last $^1/_4$ hour to allow browning.

ROASTING TIMES (TOP OVEN SET TO "ROAST" (200C/400F))
(N.B: ensure that oven is up to correct temperature before roasting.)

Bird	Weight	Approximate cooking times
Chicken	2lb/900g	45-50 minutes
	3lb/1.5kg	1 hour
	4lb/1.75kg	$1^1/_2$ hours
	5lb/2.25kg	$1^3/_4$ hours
Turkey	Weigh the bird after stuffing and allow 15 minutes per 450g/1lb + 15 minutes. Remove from oven and leave for 30 minutes to allow the flesh to firm up.	
Duck		1-$1^1/_2$ hours
Goose		$1^1/_2$ – 2 hours
Grouse		30-35 minutes
Pigeon		20-35 minutes
Partridge		30-35 minutes

....

Pheasant	45-50 minutes
Quail	15 minutes
Snipe	15 minutes
Woodcock	15 minutes

To test if cooked: pierce the thickest part of the thigh with a fine skewer, if the juices run clear the bird is cooked. Allow the bird to "rest" in the simmering oven whilst making gravy from the skimmed cooking juices.

SLOW ROASTING OF TURKEY

Prepare the turkey in the usual way, stand on the rack in the roasting tin. Cover loosely with foil and slide onto the bottom set of runners of the top oven set at "Simmer" (150C/300F), and cook for the following time:

8-10lb/3.5-4.5kg	about 9-10hours
11-15lb/5-7.25kg	about 11-12hours
16-22lb/7.5-10kg	about 13-14 hours

Remove the foil, raise the heat and brown for the last hour. Test in the usual way.

BOILED BACON AND GAMMON JOINTS

Cooking a whole piece of ham in the Rayburn is so easy and gives a moist joint, perfect for slicing. I even cook ham for friends because they love the moistness and really it takes very little effort.

Soak the joint in water for 2-3 hours to remove any saltiness. Put a trivet or an old saucer in the bottom of a suitably sized pan. Put the joint on top and pour

in enough cold water to come 2 – 3 inches up the side of the pan. Cover. Stand on the simmering end of the hot plate and bring slowly to the boil and simmer for 30 minutes. Transfer the joint to near the top of the oven set at "Simmer" (150C/300F) for the following times:

2 – 3 lb/900g – 1.5kg	2½ hours
4 – 5 lb/1.75 – 2.25kg	3 hours
6 – 7 lb/2.75 – 3 kg	3½ hours
8 – 9 lb/3.5 – 4 kg	4½ hours
10 – 11 lb/4.5 – 5kg	5½ hours
12 – 13 lb/5.5 – 6kg	6½ hours
14 – 15 lb/6.5 – 6.75kg	7½ hours
16 lb 7/25kg and over	overnight

Remove from the oven and the pan. Cool a little to handle. Strip off the skin and score the fat. Mix together a glaze of mustard and honey and spread over the surface. Stud with cloves if liked. Stand in a roasting tin with the glazing uppermost and cover the meat with foil. Hang the tin so that the meat is fairly near the top of the top oven set at "Roast" (200C/400F) and bake for 10–20 minutes, until a golden glaze has formed. Watch it closely, it may burn! Serve hot or cold.

STOCKS

Home-made stocks are easy to make in the Rayburn and they certainly taste better than the cubes. If you make a large pot full, freeze in quantities that are most useful eg 1 pints/600ml for soups, ½ pints/300ml for gravies etc.

BEEF, LAMB, CHICKEN, GAME ETC.
Place the bones of the chosen meat in a large saucepan. Add a selection of flavouring vegetables eg onions, carrots, celery – washed and chopped but not necessarily peeled. Add some peppercorns and a bouquet garni. Cover with cold water and put on a lid. Place pan on the hot part of the hot plate and bring to the boil. Transfer to the simmering end and simmer for 10 minutes. Transfer to the oven set on a low temperature "Simmer" (150C/300F) for 3–4 hours or overnight. Remove from the oven, cool and skim off excess fat. Strain through a sieve and either store in the fridge for immediate use, or freeze. For a darker stock, roast the bones in a roasting tin on the bottom set of runners of the top oven set at "Simmer" (150C/300F) for 45 minutes before proceeding as above.

VEGETABLE STOCK
Wash and chop a selection of vegetables, for example onions, carrots, leeks, celery,

turnips, broccoli. Place them in a large pan and cover with water. Add a few peppercorns and a bouquet garni of whatever fresh herbs are to hand. Bring to the boil on the hottest part of the hot plate, move to the simmering end and simmer for 10 minutes. Transfer to a low oven set at "Simmer" (150C/300F) and leave for 3–4 hours. Remove and strain through a sieve. Discard the now flavourless vegetables. Pack and freeze the cold stock, or store in the fridge for immediate use.

FISH STOCK

Place a selection of bones from unsmoked fish in a saucepan. Add washed and roughly chopped vegetables eg carrot and onion, a few peppercorns and a bouquet garni. Cover with fresh, cold water. Bring to the boil on the boiling plate, transfer to the simmering plate and simmer for 10 minutes. Move to the simmering oven and cook for 1 hour. Remove from the oven, strain through a sieve and store the cold stock in the fridge for 2 days or the freezer for no more than 2 months.

BOILED POTATOES AND OTHER ROOT VEGETABLES

Potatoes, along with other root vegetables, are best cooked in a low oven. This both conserves the stored heat in the Rayburn and prevents the kitchen filling with steam. You will need to use a pan that can be used on the hot plate and in the oven set at a low temperature, so no wooden handles. Do not be tempted to transfer the potatoes to a cold serving dish partway through cooking – the entire heat of the pan, water and vegetables is needed for successful cooking.

Wash and prepare the potatoes in the usual way. Cut them to an even size. Place in the pan, add salt to taste, cover with cold water. Put on lid and bring to the boil on the hot plate, boil for 1–2 minutes, drain off the water and then transfer to the oven set on "Simmer" (150C/300F). It is difficult to give timings, the length of cooking time will depend upon the type of potato and the size of them. Allow 30 minutes and then test. Small new potatoes and small pieces of root vegetable will take about 20 minutes. Drain the vegetables, toss in butter if liked, and serve or return to the pan and the oven to keep warm.

ROASTING VEGETABLES

Roast vegetables are always a great favourite. I know that it is fashionably healthy to eat baked potatoes instead of roast, and steamed instead of roast parsnips, but

nothing beats roast vegetables with roast meat for a special treat.

Peel and cut the vegetables to an even size. Boil for 1 minute in salted water, then drain thoroughly. While the vegetables are draining and drying put some cooking oil, lard or dripping into the roasting tin. Slide onto the floor of the top oven set on "Roast" (220C/425F). When the fat is hot tip in the dry vegetables, toss them in the fat and return to the oven, hanging the tin on one of the runners. If you are also roasting meat it may be necessary to juggle the tins during cooking. Cooking near the top will give an evenly cooked, crispy vegetable. Putting on the floor of the oven will crisp the bottom of the vegetables well. Vegetables take about 1 hour to roast. If the vegetables are put around the meat they may take longer and are often not so crispy, but they do taste wonderful!

COOKING RICE

A lot of people seem to have trouble cooking rice. Cooked in the oven of the Rayburn it is very simple and it can be kept hot without spoiling if you want to cook it slightly in advance. This is the basic method for cooking rice. Adjust the quantities to suit your needs. Use a pan that is happy on the hot plate and in the oven.

1 cup rice
1¹/₂ cups water
good pinch salt

Wash the rice in a sieve with cold, running water. Put in the saucepan. Add salt and water. Put on lid.

Bring to the boil on the hottest part of the hot plate. When boiling, transfer to either oven at "Simmer" (150C/300F).

Cook for the appropriate time. The times I have given produce a cooked, non-soggy rice. If you like rice a little more cooked, then leave it in the oven a little longer.

Remove the pan from the oven and drain the rice through a sieve – some rice will have absorbed all the water. If liked, rinse with boiling water. Serve. Alternatively if you want to keep the rice hot, return to the pan and stir in a small knob of butter. Cover and return to the bottom oven until needed.

COOKING TIMES:

White long-grain rice	12 minutes
Brown long-grain rice	20 minutes
Basmati rice	12 minutes

COOKING PASTA

Pasta needs a fast boil when cooking to prevent it sticking together. Try to use a pan that is deeper than its width. Half fill with water, add salt to taste, put the lid on and bring to the boil on the hottest part of the hot plate. Add the pasta, fresh or dried, cover and bring to the boil – watch, this will not take long! Remove the lid and start timing according to the packet instructions. It may be necessary to move the pan to the cooler end to prevent the water boiling over, but try to keep the water and pasta moving. When *al dente*, drain through a colander, return to the pan and toss in a little oil or butter to prevent sticking. Serve straight away with a chosen sauce.

PASTA SAUCES

Here are two very quick recipe for pasta, but the ideas are varied and endless.

•Fry rashers of snipped smoked bacon with a chopped onion until soft. Add to the hot pasta along with 2 beaten eggs and 1/4 pint/150ml cream beaten together. Season to taste and toss well. The hot pasta will cook the eggs;

•To the hot pasta toss in a can of chopped tomatoes, a round of chopped Mozzarella cheese, a few torn basil leaves and 2 oz/50g grated Parmesan or Sbrinz. Heat through before serving. Serve with a crisp, seasonal salad and hot herb or garlic bread.

DRIED BEANS AND PEAS

The range of dried beans available in the shops gives a whole host of flavours, colours and textures for cooking. The beans and other grains can be used for vegetarian cooking or to make meat dishes go further or just to add variety. Lentils do not need soaking before cooking, just washing and picking over. All the other pulses need to be washed, picked over and left to soak for 8-12 hours or overnight – so some forethought is necessary.

Measure out the pulses required, wash well and pick over to remove any grit. Place in a bowl and cover with cold water. Put aside to soak.

Drain the liquid from the beans. Place in a saucepan, cover with cold water and bring to the boil. Boil rapidly for 10 minutes – to prevent boiling over use a large pan and no lid at this stage. After 10 minutes rapid boil, cover and transfer to a low oven set on "Simmer" (150C/300F) until tender, 1-3 hours. The length of time depends upon the type and age of the bean. Experience will be your best judge. When cooked, use as per recipe.

BREAKFASTS

These days most families do not eat a traditional English breakfast on a daily basis, but it is lovely at weekends and holiday-time, when there is time to linger. Breakfast is so simple to cook in the Rayburn. The only part I do on the top is to boil the kettle for tea and to make the toast, unless I am serving un-sweetened Scotch pancakes with the bacon, and then I make those on the cooler end of the hot plate.

I give an outline for cooking sausages, bacon, tomato and egg, but of course you can add in any extras such as black puddings, scrambled eggs, mushrooms and kidneys. You will need the roasting tin. Lay into the slightly greased roasting tin the sausages – or the thickest food that takes the most cooking. Slide the tin onto the top set of runners of the top oven set at "Bake" (200C/400F). Cook the sausages for about 10 minutes until golden brown and sizzling. Remove the tin from the oven and lay in the bacon rashers and the tomatoes, cut in half with a cross cut in the middle to help cooking.

Turn over the sausages and return to the oven – again at the top. Cook for a further 10 minutes, this time will depend upon how you like your bacon cooked and the

thickness of the rashers. Remove the sausages to a warm plate and into the warming oven, also the tomato and bacon if cooked to your preference. If not, leave in the tin. There should be a good smearing of fat in the tin from the sausages. Whilst the tin is hot, crack in the eggs and immediately return the pan to the floor of the roasting oven. Cook for 2-3 minutes, and, depending on taste, turn the egg over and cook for 1-2 minutes. Serve on warm plates immediately.

Washing-up tip! Put the roasting pan to soak in hot soapy water straight away, otherwise that egg can be difficult to clean off.

TOAST
New owners often look for the grill on a Rayburn for somewhere to do their toast. It is simple. The bread is placed directly on the hot plate on the cooler end and is turned over with a metal or wooden fish slice.

PORRIDGE
We love porridge in the winter and it is a great favourite with a variety of toppings. I have to say that lashings of soft brown sugar comes top of the list, though I like fruit or salt — my husband favours yoghurt. This is the easiest breakfast dish to prepare, though if you are an infrequent maker of porridge you may need to leave a reminder on the breakfast table that some is in the oven! I have given a recipe for 4, but I do know some people who make individual portions in a small cereal bowl with a saucer on top as a lid.

1 cup rolled porridge oats
1 cup water
1 cup milk
pinch salt

Put all the ingredients into a small saucepan, cover with a lid, put in the low, idling oven overnight. Stir and serve with milk or cream and your favourite flavouring.

YOGHURT
Homemade yoghurt is very easy with the Rayburn supplying a constant, even temperature. If you and your family eat a lot of yoghurt it is certainly worth making. Of course you can add a variety of flavourings when it is made — fruits, jams, honey, nuts or simply use plain in savoury dishes or as a substitute for cream. Do not be tempted to use your own homemade yoghurt as a starter for a new batch, it is always safer to start with a small pot of commercial yoghurt. You can use either ordinary yoghurt or Greek style — they use different cultures so

will give you a different flavour.

1 pint/575ml carton long-life milk – whole or skimmed
1 tbsp plain yoghurt
1 tbsp dried milk powder – this thickens

Use very clean utensils. Mix the yoghurt and milk powder together in a bowl. Warm the milk – I stand mine in a jug on top of the Rayburn. Do not overheat the milk, this will kill the yoghurt bacteria. The milk should be warm to the touch. Blend the yoghurt mixture and the warm milk together.

Put a folded tea-towel or trivet beside the lids. Put the bowl containing the yoghurt mixture in the colander. Cover with a plate and leave 12 hours or overnight. The yoghurt should be set, thick and creamy. Store in the fridge.

CAKES

During my Rayburn demonstrations I have heard so many people say "I am told you cannot make a cake in a Rayburn." Nothing could be further from the truth, it is just a matter of knowing HOW to make a cake in a Rayburn.

If you are planning to bake only cakes, set the top oven temperature to the appropriate recipe temperature or to "Bake" (180C/350F) and bake the cake in the usual way. However, if the oven is hot for some other baking you will need to use the cold plain shelf to diffuse the heat from the top of the oven and allow the cake to cook through without burning.

Each Rayburn should have a large plain baking sheet, made of aluminium, and known as the cold plain shelf. Cold is the most important word here. Store this shelf, not in the oven, but in a cool cupboard. The cold shelf is put in above cakes or biscuits to reduce the top heat, and allow the cake to cook through without burning. Always allow rising space and air circulation space – usually 2 runners above the oven shelf. If you are doing a large baking session take the shelf out periodically to allow it to cool down and therefore become effective again. The cold plain shelf can be used as an oven shelf and of course food such as scones can be put above it when it is being used as a cold shelf.

BREAD AND YEAST COOKERY

Bread and yeast based dishes are so easy and successful using the Rayburn, not just because the top oven, when really hot, is so good for baking bread, but because the steady heat is perfect for warming and rising the bread dough. For a quick bread mix and for a store-cupboard standby the easy blend yeast in measured sachets is easy to use and quick. However, if you have time, try using fresh yeast and let the dough rise twice for a fuller flavour and better texture. Fresh yeast can be bought from health shops, bakers and the fresh-bake counters in supermarkets. Store in a plastic box in the fridge for about 10 days – should it go runny or smell rancid throw away and start with new yeast.

The choice of flour is largely personal. Organic flour comes in brown and white for bread making, or standard strong white or brown can be used, or a mixture of both. Special flours such as rye or granary may need to be bought at more specialist food shops. The quantities of liquids given in the recipes can only be guidelines because all flours vary in the amount of liquid they absorb. Try to make the dough as moist as possible, without being too sticky to handle, this will give a better finished product.

The main problem with breadmaking is trying not to kill the yeast. I warm the liquid by standing it on top of the Rayburn, that way it will be at blood heat and no hotter – it should be warm to the touch only. If the liquid is too hot the yeast will be killed before it can do its work! I have given a few basic recipes, but once you have mastered the art of breadmaking you can enjoy trying out new ideas and new recipes from other books.

PRESERVES

Home-made jams and chutneys are easy to make, though a little time consuming. Quite a lot of the cooking can be done in the oven set at a low temperature or cooked gently on the simmering end of the hot plate, which removes the need to watch the preserving pan all the time and prevents burning on the bottom of the pan. Jams or chutneys make wonderful presents, particularly when presented with an attractive label or in a pretty jar.

I am giving an outline for basic methods of preservation, for more detail HMSO publish Home Preservation of Fruit and Vegetables which is a really good reference book. Alternatively, my few recipes will give you the basic method and other recipes can be used. A good, large preserving pan will be needed. I use a large deep

catering pan with a lid. With mine I can get the jam boiling well without too much spitting. The lid is useful when cooking slowly in the low oven. Collect jam jars with good, clean lids. I put mine through the dishwasher and keep them ready with their lids on. They only need warming in the lower oven when needed. Labels and wax discs are needed.

When making jam or marmalade here are a few basic tops: Some fruit that needs slightly longer cooking, for instance, apricots, can be cooked in the low oven until softened. Choose a granulated or preserving sugar and always make sure it is dissolved before bringing to the boil, to prevent it crystallising.

To test for a set, remove the boiling jam from the heat after 10-15 minutes rapid boil. Put about 1 teaspoon of jam on a cold plate. Chill the sample for 1-2 minutes. If the surface wrinkles when pushed with the finger, the setting point has been reached. If the setting point has not been reached, boil again for 2-3 minutes and re-test. Too much boiling will give a syrupy jam. Cool the jam in the pan for a few minutes to prevent fruit rising to the top of the jar. Put the wax discs and lids on when the jam is either first put in the jar or when cold. Clean and label the jars when cold. Store in a cool, dark place.

Chutney is easily made in the Rayburn. The long, slow cooking which gives chutney its characteristic texture is done in the oven set on "Simmer". Again, a good sized preserving pan is useful, and as the chutney is not boiled rapidly the pan can be about 2/3 full. Jar lids need to be coated to prevent corrosion by the vinegar. Warm in the simmering oven before filling. Brown and white sugar can be used. Dark brown sugar will give a darker chutney and a rich flavour. Similarly dark malt vinegar will colour the chutney, while for a lighter pickle you can use white wine vinegar.

BOTTLING FRUIT

Bottling fruit has become fashionable again. It is much easier to use a jar of fruit for a quick pudding than thaw out fruit from the freezer. Do not be tempted to bottle vegetables, as the temperature in the Rayburn is not hot enough to make this safe. Use a Kilner jar for bottling – replacing the rubber rings or metal tops after each use. Check that the jar is in good condition – don't use any with chips. Wash and rinse the jars well. Choose fruit that is ripe, but not mushy or over-soft and bruised. For large fruits such as peaches, try to choose fruits of a similar size.

Bottling is done in the oven set at mid-simmer or 130C/250F, and is very simple if the following method is used.

1. Line the large roasting tin with a few sheets of newspaper.

2. Stand in the clean jars – side by side but not touching.

3. Place tin and jars in the simmering oven for a few minutes to warm.

4. Prepare a syrup, about 8 oz/225g sugar to 1 pint/600ml water; the strength depends upon personal taste.

5. Remove the roasting tin from the oven and pack the jars with the prepared and washed fruits.

6. Pour in the boiling syrup, tapping each jar to bring air bubbles to the surface. Fill to within 1 inch/2.5cm of the top.

7. Fit on the lids – DO NOT SCREW ON ANY BANDS – this may cause the jar to explode.

8. Slide the roasting tin on the bottom set of runners of the simmering oven and heat for the following length of time.

1-2 jars	1 hour
3-6 jars	2-3 hours
7-10 jars	2½ – 4 hours

The jars at the back will cook faster than the front. Look for tiny air bubbles and the fruit rising to the surface will indicate that the fruit is cooked. Light fruits may discolour if more than 6 bottles are done at a time – due to lower cooking temperatures. Remove from the oven, check that the rings and lids are in place – screw down firmly. Cool completely before checking to see if they are sealed – remove the screw band and lift the jar with the lid. If it remains secure wipe and rescrew the band. Store in a dark place.

CHRISTMAS

So many people seem to have their Rayburn fitted or "inherit" a Rayburn just before Christmas. My Rayburn workshop days in November and December and demonstrations at the Rayburn shop before Christmas are always over-subscribed.

A lot of people worry about the size of the oven/turkey, losing heat, getting everything done in time. Personally, I like to enjoy a relaxed Christmas Day, so I prepare as much as possible the day before. All the exact details for cooking will be found with each recipe. Give the temperature a little boost the night before to give extra capacity. A large turkey can be cooked slowly overnight, though of course the cooking method and time will have to be calculated according to the

size of the turkey, your final planned eating time and what time you go to bed on Christmas Eve. A smaller 12 lb turkey will fit into the small roasting tin, giving room for another tin for the roast vegetables.

• When the turkey is out of the oven and resting in a warm spot for 15 minutes before carving that is the time to crisp any roast vegetables – either at the very top of the roasting oven or directly on the floor.
• Christmas puddings can be put on to steam for half an hour on the simmering end of the hot plate and then transferred to the bottom oven if it is cast iron, or allow the pudding to steam gently on the top. Puddings in the oven will sit happily until needed.
• If the vegetables are ready and you are not, drain, put on a knob of butter and put into the serving dishes and into the warming lower oven to keep warm. All this should leave ample heat to quickly boil or steam green vegetables and to make the gravy.
• Sauces like breadsauce can be made early or the day before and warmed through in the lower oven. With the quantity of food being cooked there is rarely space to warm plates and dishes. This is where I find a hot tray useful, or even a large washing-up bowl full of really hot water to put dishes and plates in.
• As a last resort, if cooking is taking a little longer than planned, have some nibbles handy.

If this is your first Christmas with a Rayburn, keep everything as simple as possible. Starters can be cold and prepared in advance. A second pudding could also be cold. Whatever, RELAX.

SOUPS AND STARTERS

ROAST NUTS

FOR NIBBLES

....

I find assorted nuts done this way are really moreish to hand round with drinks. If you like spicy nuts, stir in 1 teaspoon Garam Masala with the salt. A jar of these makes an attractive present. It is also a good way to use up bits of left-over nuts, especially after Christmas!

Take an assortment of nuts eg pecans, brazils, walnuts, cashews, whole almonds and some sea salt

Lay the nuts on a baking tray. Place on the oven shelf, about mid-way, in the top oven set on "Bake" (200C/400F). Roast until slightly browning. Watch! They will burn quickly! Remove from the oven and immediately toss in some sea salt. The nuts should be slightly oily so that the salt will stick. If they seem dry, toss in 1 teaspoon olive oil with the salt. Serve warm or cold. If putting in a jar, allow to cool completely before putting the lid on.

GOUGERE
CHEESE CHOUX PUFFS

....

I often make these as a hand-around starter for a supper party. They are best straight from the oven, but can also be eaten cold. The top oven needs to be set at "Roast" (220C/425F) for their baking so if the oven needs to be full, bake in advance and warm through before serving.

3 oz/75g plain white flour
¹/₄ tsp salt
shake of pepper
2 oz/50g butter – cut into cubes
2 eggs – beaten
3 oz/75g grated Gruyère

Sieve flour, salt and pepper onto a sheet of greaseproof paper.

Put the butter into a saucepan with ¼ pint/150ml water. Stand on the simmering end of the hot plate and allow the butter to melt. Bring to the boil, tip in the flour and beat well with a wooden spoon until the mixture leaves the sides of the pan clean. Cool.

Beat in the eggs – I use an electric mixer – until the mixture is smooth and glossy. Add the grated cheese and beat well.

Grease a baking tray. Spoon out about 12 dessert spoons of mixture. Bake on the third set of runners from the top in the top oven for 15-20 minutes. Check that the puffs are not browning too much – if they are move the oven shelf to the floor of the oven. If not too brown leave nearer the top. Bake for a further 10 minutes. Serve warm or cold.

Makes about 12.
....

CROUSTADES

....

These are easy to make "nibbles", perfect for pre-dinner drinks or as a stand-up starter. Prepare ahead and bake as needed.

15 slices white bread – from a sliced loaf
4 oz/100g butter
4 oz/100g blue cheese – Stilton or Roquefort

TO FINISH:
2 oz/50g melted butter
2 tsp caraway seeds

Cut the crusts from the bread. Roll each slice with a rolling pin to flatten.

Cream the butter and the crumbled cheese together, spread this butter mixture over the bread slices. Roll up tightly. Cut each roll in half.

Grease the small roasting tin. Pack in the bread rolls tightly, with the ends of the slices underneath.

Brush the rolls with the melted butter. Sprinkle on the caraway seeds.

Hang the roasting tin on the top runners of the top oven set at "Roast" (220C/425F) for about 15 minutes until golden brown. Serve warm.

Makes 15.
....

PATE MAISON

Pâtés are quick and easy to make, especially if you have a food processor or an electric mincer. They taste much nicer than commercial varieties and are much more economical. This is a coarse pâté, good for picnics and cold lunches with tasty bread or toast.

2 lb/900g streaky pork rashers
¹/₂ lb/225g pig's liver
4 oz/100g streaky bacon
1 lb/450g minced lamb or veal
2 tbsp brandy
4 tbsp white wine
2 cloves garlic – peeled
ground black pepper
4 juniper berries – crushed
1 tsp salt

Coarsely mince the pork rashers, liver and bacon. Combine in a mixing bowl all the ingredients and stir well to mix.

Put the mixture into a 2 pint capacity terrine or loaf tin.

Set the oven to "Simmer" (150C/300F). Put the shelf on the bottom set of runners in the top oven and slide in the prepared pâté. Cook for about 2 hours, or until the pâté has shrunk from the sides of the tin. Cool and chill before slicing.

CHICKEN TERRINE

Chicken makes a lighter pâté, both in colour and flavour. A chicken terrine is good to serve with a good crisp salad and a variety of breads for lunch, or for a cold buffet table.

2 lb/900g boneless chicken thighs
1 small onion – peeled
1 lb/450g sausagemeat
1 level tsp salt pepper
1 tbsp finely chopped parsley
1 egg
8 rashers unsmoked streaky bacon

Either mince or process the chicken and onion. Combine in a mixing bowl with the sausagemeat, salt, pepper, parsley and egg. Mix thoroughly. Stretch out the rashers of bacon with the back of a knife blade. Use 4 rashers to line a 2½ pint/1 litre capacity terrine or loaf tin. Spoon in the pâté mixture, tap the tin on the work surface to remove any air bubbles. Lay on the remaining bacon rashers. Cover tightly with foil.

Set the oven at "Simmer" (150C/300F). Put the shelf on the bottom set of runners in the top oven and slide in the prepared pâté. Cook for about 2 hours or until the pâté has shrunk from the side of the tin. Cool and chill before slicing.

HERB PATE

....

This is an economical pâté to make for informal lunches or picnics. It is also popular in school packed lunches.

1 lb/450g pig's liver
12 oz/350g streaky bacon
1 small onion,
chopped pinch black pepper
³/₄ level tsp ground coriander
pinch grated nutmeg ¹/₄ level tsp
dried mixed herbs or
2 tbsp fresh chopped herbs
1 egg, beaten

Wash the liver and trim off the bacon rind. Fry the bacon rind in a pan on the simmering end of the hot plate until the fat runs, then discard the rind. Fry the onion in the fat until transparent.

Mince the liver and bacon 3 times, or process until fairly fine. Mix in the onion, pepper, coriander, nutmeg and herbs. Add the egg and mix well.

Grease and line a 2lb loaf tin. Spoon the mixture in. Cover with foil. Stand the loaf in the roasting tin. Pour round hot water to come half way up tin. Hang the tin from the bottom runner of the top oven set at "Simmer" (150C/300F) and cook for 1¹/₂ hours.

Remove from oven and weight down the top with weights or baked bean tins until cold.

VEGETABLE TERRINE

....

Attractively striped in cream and orange layers, this striking vegetable terrine is so easy to make and yet looks stunning sliced for a starter. Serve with a vinaigrette dressing which has 2 teaspoons tomato purée added.

1 large cauliflower – florets washed
1¹/₂ lb/675g carrots – peeled and sliced
salt and pepper
¹/₂ pint/300ml double cream
2 eggs
¹/₄ tsp freshly grated nutmeg
¹/₄ tsp ground coriander

In separate saucepans cook the cauliflower and carrots in boiling, salted water. Cook the cauliflower until just tender and the carrots until well cooked. Drain well.

Purée the cauliflower in a blender or processor until smooth. Transfer to a bowl. Purée the carrot in the same way and put in a separate bowl. Add 1 egg and half the cream to each bowl. Beat in well. Season with salt and pepper. Stir the grated nutmeg into the cauliflower mixture. Stir the coriander into the carrot mixture.

Grease a 2¹/₂ pint loaf tin or terrine tin. Put half the cauliflower in the base of the tin, level. Gently cover with a layer of half the carrot purée, followed by the remaining cauliflower and then the remaining carrot mixture. Tap the tin on the work surface to remove any air bubbles.

Cover the tin tightly with foil. Put the shelf on the bottom set of runners of the top oven set at "Simmer" (150C/300F). Put in the terrine. Bake for 1 hour or until firm.

Remove the terrine from the oven and allow to cool slightly before turning out on to a serving plate. Slice with a sharp knife and serve with a little tomato flavoured vinaigrette. Serve hot or cold.

Serves 8-10.
....

CREAMY MUSHROOMS

Commercially grown button mushrooms often do not have much flavour. This recipe adds gentle flavouring. Serve the mushrooms on a bed of lettuce and chicory with maybe some bread to mop up any juices.

1 oz/25g butter
1 lb/450g button mushrooms – wiped clean
1 tbsp flour
¹/₄ pint/150ml fresh milk
2 tbsp wholegrain mustard
2 tbsp fresh tarragon – chopped or ¹/₂ tsp dried tarragon
3 tbsp soured cream

Melt the butter in a large saucepan or frying pan on the simmering end of the hot plate. Add the mushrooms and cook for 2 minutes. Stir in the flour and then the milk. Heat, stirring continuously, until the sauce thickens and is smooth. Simmer for 1-2 minutes.

Stir in the mustard, tarragon and soured cream. Serve hot on a bed of chicory, and lettuce.

Serves 4.

ASPARAGUS SOUP

....

The thicker stemmed asparagus can be used for this soup as it has more flavour. This soup bears no resemblance to packet or canned asparagus soup! Serve chilled on a warm summer evening or gently warmed if the weather is chillier.

1¹/₂ lb/675g asparagus
salt and pepper
2 small onions – peeled and chopped
1 oz/25g butter
2¹/₂ pints/1.5 litres
chicken stock
5 fl oz/225ml single cream

Cut the tips off the asparagus and simmer gently in boiling, salted water until tender. Drain and refresh in cold water. Drain and reserve.

Trim the stalks of the asparagus and cut into 2 inch lengths. Melt the butter in a large saucepan on the simmering end of the hot plate, add the asparagus stalks and the onion, stir, cover and cook for 5-10 minutes until soft but not browning. Add the stock and seasoning. Bring to the boil, cover and transfer to the oven if it is set on a low heat or simmer on the cooler end of the hot plate for about 45 minutes or until the asparagus is cooked.

Pass the soup through a blender or processor and then through a sieve to remove any woody stalk. Stir in the cream. Chill or warm through gently.

Serve garnished with the reserved asparagus tips.

Serves 6-8.
....

C O C K - A - L E E K I E   S O U P

A traditional Scottish soup that is more of a meal in a dish than a starter soup. A little beef can also be added for a more robust flavour.

¹/₂ oz/15g butter
2 chicken quarters
12 oz/350g leeks, trimmed
2 pints/1 litre chicken stock
1 bouquet garni
salt and pepper
6 ready-to-eat prunes, halved and stoned

Melt the butter in a large oven-proof saucepan and fry the chicken until golden brown.

Chop off the white part of the leek and dice. Reserve the green part. Wash all the leek well. Add the white part to the pan and cook until soft, about 5 minutes.

Add the stock, bouquet garni and seasoning to taste. Bring to the boil, cover and cook gently either on the coolest end of the hot plate or in the oven set on "Simmer" (150C/300F) for 1 hour or until the chicken is tender.

Shred the remaining green leek, add to the pan with the prunes and continue cooking for a further half an hour.

To serve, remove the chicken, cut the meat into large pieces and discard the skin and bone. Put the meat into warmed soup bowls and pour over the soup. Serve hot.

Serves 4 as a meal.

PARSNIP SOUP

....

This is a thick, winter-warming soup. Serve with home-made bread for lunch or as a supper dish.

1 oz/25g butter
1 large onion – peeled and chopped
1 level tsp curry powder (medium strength)
1 lb/450g parsnips – peeled and diced
¹/₂ lb/225g potatoes – peeled and diced
2 pints/1200ml chicken or vegetable stock

Melt the butter in a large saucepan. Toss the onion in the butter and cook over a gentle heat until soft. Stir in the curry powder and cook for 1-2 minutes.

Add the diced parsnips and potatoes. Stir well, add the stock. Bring to the boil.

Cover and transfer to the top oven set at "Simmer" (150C/300F) or continue to simmer on the cool end of the hot plate for about 1 hour or until parsnips are soft.

Remove from the oven and pass through a food processor of liquidiser.

Season to taste. Heat through and serve with whirls of cream.

Serves 6.
....

T O M A T O   A N D   S W E E T   P E P P E R   S O U P

....

I do not usually like tomato soup, but the addition of the red peppers makes this soup rich and sweet. This is a good winter soup because tinned tomatoes are used. The recipe will give 8 good portions.

2 oz/50g butter
12 oz/350g onion – chopped
2 large red peppers – deseeded and sliced
2 tbsp tomato purée
1 14oz/400g can tomatoes
2 tbsp chopped parsley
1 level tsp sugar
1 bayleaf
¼ tsp dried basil
¼ tsp dried thyme
2 ½ pints/1500ml light stock,
chicken or vegetable salt and pepper

Melt butter in a large saucepan on the cooler end of the hot plate. Gently fry the onion and pepper until soft.

Stir in the remaining ingredients, bring to the boil. Transfer to the pan to the coolest end of the hot plate or to the top oven set at "Simmer" (150C/300F) for 30-45 minutes.

Purée the soup in a blender or processor. Warm through and adjust the seasoning.

Serves 8-10.

....

CELERY SOUP

....

This is one of my favourite soups.

1 head celery – cleaned and sliced
1 onion – chopped
1 oz/25g butter
1 oz/25g flour
³/₄ pint/450ml chicken or vegetable stock
1 blade mace
salt and pepper
¹/₂ pint/300ml milk
a little cream for serving

Melt the butter in a pan on the simmering end of the hot plate, stir in the chopped celery and onion and cook until soft but not coloured.

Add the flour and stir well, cooking gently for 1 minute. Gradually add the stock, mace and a little salt and pepper.

Bring to the boil, cover and place in the top oven set on "Simmer" (150c/300F), or simmer gently on the simmering end of the hot plate for 30 minutes.

Remove the pan from the oven and blend the soup. Rinse the pan, return the soup to the pan and add the milk. Heat through until piping hot. Taste and season.

Serve in warm bowls with a swirl of cream.

Makes enough for 6 small or 4 large portions.
....

MAIN COURSE

FISH

FISH CAKES

Fish cakes made at home can be full of flavour and appeal to all the family. Ring the changes with different fish and herbs. Salmon and dill can be used to make something special. The herbs also give an attractive appearance.

10 oz/275g haddock, skinned and boned
1 tbsp lemon juice
1 tbsp Worcestershire sauce
1 tbsp creamed horseradish
4 fl oz milk
1 tbsp fresh chives, snipped
1 tbsp fresh parsley, chopped
12 oz/350g maincrop potatoes,
cooked and mashed
2 oz/50g fresh breadcrumbs

Place the fish and milk in an ovenproof dish, cover with foil and put to poach on the middle set of runners of the top oven set at "Bake" (200V/400F) for 10-15 minutes, until just flaking.

Remove the fish from the oven, put in a bowl and flake fairly finely. Add the mashed potatoes, parsley, chives, horseradish, Worcestershire sauce and lemon juice. Mix all together, adding the poaching milk as needed to bind the fish cakes together. Shape into 4 fish cakes and coat with breadcrumbs. If time allows, cover and chill for half an hour.

Smear a little cooking oil in the small roasting tin. Put to heat on the floor of the top oven. When the oil is hazing, put in the fish cakes and return the tin to the floor of the oven. Cook for 5 minutes, turn over and cook for a further 5 minutes until golden brown and sizzling hot. Serve immediately.

Serves 4.

BAKED MACKEREL WITH GOOSEBERRY SAUCE

A lovely summer dish that can be eaten all year round if you put some gooseberries in the freezer for the winter. The tang of the gooseberries goes well with this oily fish – often a good buy at the fishmongers. For a smooth sauce remove the pips by sieving.

¹/₂ oz/12g butter
8 oz/225g gooseberries, topped and tailed
4 mackerel, cleaned, with heads removed
salt and pepper
lemon juice to taste
1 egg, beaten

Melt the butter in a saucepan on the simmering end of the hot plate, stir in the gooseberries and cover with a tightly fitting lid. Heat through for a couple of minutes and either cook gently on the hot plate or transfer to the shelf on the bottom set of runners in the top oven set at "Roast" (250C (450F). Cook for about 20-30 minutes until tender.

Season the mackerel inside and out with salt, pepper and lemon juice. Make two or three diagonal slashes in the skin on each side of the fish. Place on the rack inside the roasting tin. Slide the tin onto the second set of runners from the top of the top oven and grill for 15-20 minutes, turning it half-way through, until tender.

Purée the gooseberries in a processor or sieve. Pour the purée into a clean pan, beat in the egg and heat gently, stirring. Season to taste.

Place the mackerel on warmed serving plates and spoon the sauce alongside.

Serves 4.

FISHY PASTA

....

This fish sauce is served with tagliatelle, but it can also be used as a base for a fish pie. Top with finely sliced, par-boiled potatoes or mashed potatoes and bake in the top oven set on "Bake" (200C/400F) for 20-30 minutes until piping hot and golden brown.

1 lb/450g haddock or cod fillet
8 oz/225g smoked haddock or cod fillets
2 oz/50g butter
6 oz/175g mushrooms – diced
1½ oz/35g flour
½ pint/300ml milk
¼ pint/150ml water
6 spring onions – sliced
2 tbsp fresh parsley – chopped
4 oz/100g peeled prawns – thawed if frozen
salt and pepper
1¼ lb/550g tagliatelli verdi

Place the fish in a roasting tin with the milk and water. Cover lightly with foil, hang on the third set of runners from the top of the top oven set at "Bake" (200C/400F) and poach for 15-20 minutes until cooked. Heat water for pasta and cook according to instructions.

Melt the butter in a saucepan and saute the mushrooms until cooked. Remove to a plate with a slotted spoon and keep warm in the bottom warming oven. Stir in the flour, cook for 1 minute and then gradually beat in the fish cooking liquor. Stir and boil the sauce, then add the mushrooms, spring onions, parsley and seasoning. Simmer gently for 5 minutes.

Meanwhile remove the skin and bones from the fish and then flake the flesh into largeish pieces. Gently fold the fish and prawns into the sauce. Cover and keep warm in the simmering oven while the pasta is cooking.

Drain the pasta and top with the fish sauce.

Serves 4-6.

....

SALMON FILO TART

The filling in this rises like a soufflé and looks stunning. Serve with new potatoes and baby vegetables.

4 oz/100g butter
4 oz/100g filo pastry
8 oz/225g salmon
¹/₂ pint/300ml milk
1 bay leaf
1¹/₂ oz/35g plain flour
4 eggs – separated
2 tbsp chopped fresh dill
1 tbsp chopped chives
3 oz/75g grated Gruyère
salt and pepper

Melt half the butter and brush base and sides of 9-10 inch/23-25cm flan dish with it. Lay the pastry out on the worktop and brush the top sheet with melted butter. Lay a sheet of buttered pastry over the base of the flan dish. Continue in this way until the dish is lined. Cover with cling film. Chill.

Put the salmon in an ovenproof dish. Pour on the milk, add the bay leaf. Put the oven shelf on the bottom set of runners of the top oven set at "Roast" (250C/475F) and slide in the salmon dish and cook the salmon for 15-20 minutes. Drain, reserving milk. Skin the salmon, remove the bones and flake the flesh.

Melt the remaining butter in a saucepan. Add the flour and the reserved milk, stirring well. Bring to the boil, and simmer until thick and smooth. Off the heat, beat in the egg yolks, herbs, cheese and seasoning.

Whisk the egg whites until softly stiff. Fold them into sauce, along with the salmon. Take the sling film off the pastry case and fill it with the sauce.

Place the flan dish on the floor of the hot top oven and bake for 25-30 minutes, until risen and golden. Serve warm.

Serves 6.

P L A I C E   B A K E D   W I T H   C H E E S E

Use a finely grated mature cheese such as Sbrinz or Parmesan for the best taste and appearance. The plaice can easily be replaced with lemon or Dover Sole, whichever is used it needs to be thin fillets.

4 large fillets of plaice
¹/₂ oz/15g butter
3 tbsp dry white wine
juice of ¹/₂ lemon
3 oz/75g grated Sbrinz or Parmesan
black pepper

Butter a large, shallow, oven-proof dish. Wash and pat dry the fish. Season it on both sides with the pepper and lay it out in the dish.

Pour the wine and lemon juice round the fish and sprinkle with the finely grated cheese.

Set the oven to "Bake" (200C/400F) and put the shelf on the bottom set of runners of the top oven, slide in the dish of fish and bake for 15-20 minutes until the fish is cooked and lightly golden brown.

Serves 4.

KEDGEREE

....

This is a traditional breakfast dish, but I like it for supper. The quantities can be increased easily for a crowd and can be assembled at the last minute. Good for a brunch party.

1 lb/450g smoked haddock fillets
1 lemon – sliced
pepper
3 eggs – hard-boiled and shelled
12 oz/350g cooked long-grain rice,
brown or white (about 5 oz/150g uncooked)
2 oz/50g butter – softened
2 tbsp parsley - chopped
3 fl oz/75ml single cream

Place the fish in an oven-proof dish and cover with water. Sprinkle with pepper and lay on half the lemon slices. Set the top oven to "Bake" (200C/400F) and put the oven shelf on the second set of runners from the bottom. Slide in the fish and cook for 15-20 minutes, depending upon the size and shape of the fillets, until the fish is tender.

Drain the fish, remove and discard the skin and bone. Flake the fish. Chop the eggs.

Rinse out the ovenproof dish, mix in it the rice, butter, fish, eggs, parsley and cream. Cover with foil and return to the oven to heat through – about 10-15 minutes.

Stir and garnish with lemon slices and a little parsley.

Serves 4-6.
....

SAVOURY FISH CRUMBLE

Savoury crumbles are delicious for family meals. Ring the changes with different fish – cod, haddock, whiting. This can be prepared in advance and reheated in the oven until hot right through and golden on the top.

1-1 ¹/₂ lb/450-700g white fish
milk for poaching
1 tbsp oil
4 leeks – trimmed, washed and sliced
4 sticks celery – scrubbed and sliced
6 oz/150g button mushrooms – wiped and halved
4 hard-boiled eggs – peeled and quartered
³/₄ pint/450ml milk
1 oz/40g flour
1 ¹/₂oz/40g butter
salt and pepper

CRUMBLE TOPPING
6 oz/150g wholemeal breadcrumbs
4 oz/100g cheese – grated
2 tbsp chopped fresh herbs or 2 tsp mixed dried herbs
1 oz/25g butter

Poach the fish in the milk until cooked, about 10-15 minutes in the top oven set at "Bake" (200C/400F). In a saucepan heat the oil and gently fry the leeks and celery. When softening, add the mushrooms and cook until soft. Remove any skin and bones from the fish. Put the fish mixture into a shallow ovenproof dish and add the eggs and vegetables. Make a white sauce with the milk, flour and butter. Season and pour over the fish. Mix the breadcrumbs, grated cheese and herbs together and sprinkle over. Dot with slivers of butter and bake, with the oven shelf on the second set of runners from the bottom, for 30-40 minutes until golden brown.

Serves 4.

MEAT, POULTRY AND GAME

ITALIAN-STYLE STEAK

....

This steak will look more professional if it is cooked in the ridged cast-iron pan, but this is not essential. Cooking in the oven not only saves heat wastage but all smells disappear up the chimney.

4 thin-cut rump steaks
2 cloves garlic – peeled and crushed
salt and pepper
1 lb/450g tomatoes – skinned and chopped
1 tbsp fresh basil – chopped
2 tbsp parsley – chopped
olive oil

Heat the pan on the floor of the top oven set at "Roast" (250C/475F) or use the hot plate until it is really hot, 5-8 minutes. When hot, place in the steaks and fry quickly for 2-3 minutes browning on both sides.

Add garlic, salt and pepper. Stir in the tomatoes and herbs and a little olive oil if necessary. Cook for 3-5 minutes until the tomatoes are softened but still holding their shape.

Serve immediately with new potatoes and green salad.

Serves 4.
....

BEEF IN STOUT

....

This easy to prepare casserole has a rich, tasty gravy. The stewing steak benefits from long, slow cooking.

2 lb/900g stewing steak – cubed
¹/₂ oz/12g butter
1 tbsp vegetable oil
4 medium onions – sliced
8 oz/225g button mushrooms – wiped and halved
salt and pepper
2 tbsp flour
¹/₂ pint/300ml Stout
1 bay leaf 1 tsp
soft brown sugar

Heat the butter and oil in a large, flameproof casserole and brown the meat. Remove the meat to a plate.

Add the onion and cook until softening. Stir in the mushrooms, adding a little more oil if necessary. Stir in the flour and a seasoning of salt and pepper.

Return the meat to the casserole dish, pour in the stout, add the bay leaf and sugar. Stir well, cover and bring to a gentle boil. Boil for 2-3 minutes then transfer to the top oven set at "Simmer" (150C (300F) for about 3 hours or until the meat is tender. Serve with creamy mashed potatoes and lightly cooked carrots.

Serves 6.
....

CLASSIC BEEF CASSEROLE

....

The Rayburn at a low idling heat is ideal for cooking casseroles slowly, as it develops rich flavours and tenderises the meat. This recipe has a strong French influence and can easily be adapted to suit whatever ingredients are to hand. Serve with crisp baked potatoes and very fresh green vegetables or a crispy salad to follow.

2 lb/900g good braising steak or skirt, cut into large squares
6 oz/175g unsmoked streaky bacon – in the piece if possible, diced
2 onions – peeled and sliced
2 carrots – peeled and sliced
2 tomatoes – skinned and sliced
2 cloves garlic – peeled
bouquet garni
2 tbsp olive oil
¹/₄ pint/150ml red wine

In the bottom of a flameproof casserole pour the olive oil, then place in the bacon and prepared vegetables. Lay the meat on top. Bury the garlic and the bouquet garni in the centre.

Stand the casserole, uncovered, on the simmering end of the hot plate to start the cooking.

After about 10-15 minutes put the wine in a small pan on the boiling plate. When boiling set the wine alight and allow the alcohol to burn off. When the flames have died down pour the wine over the casserole. Cover with a lid and allow the casserole to come to the boil. Transfer to the top oven set on "Simmer" (150C/300F) for 3 hours.

To serve, dish the meat, bacon and vegetables onto a warm serving platter. Skim off most of the fat from the liquid and remove the bouquet garni. Heat the sauce to bubbling on the simmering end of the hot plate and pour over the meat.

Serves 6-8.
....

BASIC BOLOGNESE SAUCE

....

This is such a useful standby. Make a large batch and freeze in portions. I use this meat sauce with spaghetti and as a filling for lasagne. Cook gently in a low oven for a good flavour and tender meat. In our family we like a rich tomato sauce, so I use creamed tomatoes or passata, but canned tomatoes can be used.

1 lb/450g lean minced beef
1 tbsp olive oil
1 onion – chopped
4 oz/100g sliced mushrooms
1 clove garlic – crushed
1 carton creamed tomatoes
¹/₄ pint/150ml red wine
1 bay leaf
¹/₂ tsp dried oregano or about 10 basil leaves, torn

Heat the olive oil in a saucepan on the simmering end of the hot plate, add the onion and cook until soft but not browned. Add the mushrooms and the garlic and cook until softening. Remove to a plate.

Move the pan to the hottest end of the hot plate, add the meat, break up and brown, stirring. Return to the cooler end, stir in the mushroom and onion mixture, tomatoes, red wine, bay leaf and herbs. Bring to the boil, stirring. Cover with a lid and transfer to a low oven set on "Simmer" (150C/300F) for 1 hour.

Serve with cooked spaghetti and grated Swiss Sbrinz or use as a filling for lasagne.

Serves 4.
....

LASAGNE

....

This dish can be made in advance, which is useful as it can be fairly time-consuming to make. The recipe uses the usual meat sauce, but lasagne can also be made with fish or vegetables – pre-cook either and add to a creamy sauce before layering with the lasagne. Finish off with the sauce and cheese topping. Lasagnes are easier to make and serve in an oblong dish.

Meat sauce using 1lb/450g meat – as for basic Bolognese sauce
9 oz/250g packet ready to use lasagne
³/₄ pint/450ml single cream
2 oz/50g plain flour
salt and pepper
3 oz/75g strongly flavoured, finely grated cheese eg Gruyère

Mix the flour and the cream together. Season this sauce with salt and pepper.

Butter an oblong dish. Pour a thin layer of sauce in the bottom. Layer on the sheets of lasagne followed by a layer of meat sauce. Repeat, finishing with lasagne. Pour on any remaining sauce and sprinkle with grated cheese.

Set the oven on a low "Bake" (180C/350F). Put the oven shelf on the bottom set of runners and bake for 45 minutes until firm and golden brown. If the lasagne is cooked and you are not quite ready then transfer it to the bottom oven to keep warm.

Serves 4-6.
....

QUORMA LAMB CURRY

This is more a spicy dish than a hot curry. My family like spicy, tasty food but are not keen on hot curries, so this is perfect. The curry will sit happily in a low oven for a longer time if you are delayed.

> *1 lb/450g trimmed, boned shoulder of lamb, cubed*
> *¹/₂ tbsp grated fresh root ginger*
> *salt*
> *2 oz/50g butter 1 onion,*
> *sliced 2 cloves of garlic, chopped*
> *1 tsp whole cardamom pods*
> *1 tsp whole coriander seeds*
> *1 tsp whole cloves*
> *1 tsp black peppercorns*
> *2 oz/50g creamed coconut, grated*
> *2 oz/50g double cream*
> *¹/₂ tsp ground turmeric*
> *1 tsp sugar*
> *1 fl oz/25ml lemon juice*

Mix the lamb, ginger and a little salt.

Melt the butter and sweat the onions and garlic slowly for 5 minutes.

Slit the cardamom pods and remove the black seeds. Grind to a powder with the coriander, cloves and peppercorns. Sprinkle over the onions and cook for 1 minute.

Add the meat and remaining ingredients to the pan. Mix well, cover and get piping hot on the simmering end of the hot plate.

Transfer to the top oven set at "Simmer" (150C/300F) for 1¹/₂ to 2 hours. Taste and adjust seasoning. Serve with rice.

Serves 4.

LEMON AND LAMB MEATBALLS

The lemon imparts a fresh taste to lamb. The meatballs can be made in advance and then browned and cooked when needed.

1 lb/450g minced lamb
1 onion – grated
1 potato – peeled and grated
1 egg – beaten
salt and pepper
1 tbsp chopped parsley
1 oz/25g flour
1 oz/25g butter
¼ pint/150ml light stock
finely grated rind and juice of 1 lemon
2 tsp cornflour – blended with a little water

Put the lamb, onion, potato, egg, salt and pepper and parsley in a bowl and mix well. Take tablespoons of the mixture and form into balls. Roll in flour and chill in the fridge for about half an hour.

Melt the butter in a flameproof casserole on the simmering end of the hot plate. Fry the meatballs until browned. Pour in the stock, lemon juice and rind. Cover and bring to the boil. Put the shelf on the bottom set of runners in the top oven set at "Simmer" (150C/300F). Put in the casserole, cook for 1 hour.

Return the casserole to the cool end of the hot plate. Stir in the slaked cornflour, bring to the boil, stirring to thicken the sauce.

Taste, adjust seasoning and serve.

Serves 4.

SWEET AND SOUR PORK

I love the flavours of sweet and sour pork, but I am not keen on deep-fat frying, so I make a casserole to cook the meat and add crispy vegetables towards the end of the cooking time. Serve with plain rice.

MARINADE
1 lb/450g lean pork – cut into cubes
1 tbsp dry sherry
1 tbsp light soy sauce

SAUCE
$^1/_4$ pint/150ml chicken stock
1 tbsp oil
1 tbsp soy sauce
$1^1/_2$ tbsp cider or white wine vinegar
1 tbsp sugar
1 tbsp tomato purée
$^1/_2$ green pepper – sliced finely
$^1/_2$ red pepper – sliced finely
2 carrots – sliced
4 spring onions – chopped
1 small bag bean shoots
1 tsp cornflour, blend with a little water

Toss the meat in the sherry and 1 tablespoon soy sauce. Marinate for at least half an hour to tenderise the meat and add flavour. Heat the oil in a flameproof casserole and brown the meat. Stir in the chicken stock, soy sauce, vinegar, sugar, tomato purée and carrots. Bring to the boil, put it in the oven set at "Simmer" (150C/300F) for 1 to $1^1/_2$ hours.

Return to the simmer end of the hot plate, stir in the peppers and spring onions and simmer for 10 minutes. Stir in the cornflour paste and the bean shoots. Stir well until heated through. Taste and serve.

Serves 4.

POT ROAST OF PORK WITH RED CABBAGE AND APPLE

....

Use a rolled boneless pork joint for this recipe, it will be perfect for pot roasting. Red cabbage and apple go very well together and add moistness to the pork.

3 tbsp red wine vinegar
1 small red cabbage – finely shredded
1 cooking apple – peeled, cored and sliced
1 tbsp demerara sugar
1 tbsp plain flour
salt and pepper
2 lb/900g boneless pork joint – rolled

Bring a large pan of water to the boil. Add 1 tablespoon of vinegar and the cabbage. Bring back to the boil then drain well.

Place the cabbage and apple slices in a casserole dish. Toss in the sugar, flour and remaining vinegar. Season to taste and stir well.

Sprinkle the joint with salt and pepper. Place on top of the cabbage and put the lid on.

Put the oven shelf on the bottom set of runners of the top oven set at "Bake" (180C/350F) and bake for 2 hours, until the meat is tender. Serve the pork sliced, accompanied with the cabbage and mashed potatoes.

Serves 6-8.

....

PORK CHOPS WITH CHEESE AND BEER

....

These chops are grilled and have a delicious topping. The chops can also be served plain, cooked in the same way without the topping.

4 pork loin chops
4 oz/100g good Cheddar cheese – grated
1 tsp mustard
3 tbsp brown ale

Place the rack in the roasting tin and lay on the chops. Slide the roasting tin onto the top set of runners in the top oven, set at "Roast" (230C/450F) and grill the chops for 10-12 minutes, depending upon thickness. Turn them over and cook for a further 10-12 minutes until cooked through.

Mix together the cheese, mustard and ale and spread over the chops. Return to the grill until the cheese has melted.

Serve garnished with tomato and watercress.

Serves 4.
....

PORK AND PARSNIP CASSEROLE

A truly delicious casserole if you like the taste of fresh ginger. During the slow cooking the parsnips take on the ginger flavour which goes very well with the pork. Any cut of pork can be used provided it is not too fatty.

1¹/₂ lb/675g pork
1 lb/450g parsnips
8 oz/225g small onions
2 tbsp oil
1 clove garlic
³/₄ pint/450ml light stock
1 tbsp soy sauce
1 tbsp golden syrup
2 tbsp white wine vinegar
¹/₂ inch fresh root ginger –
peeled and grated 1 level tbsp cornflour
salt and pepper

Cut parsnips into 1 inch cubes. Peel and quarter the onions, keeping the roots intact. Peel the garlic.

Heat the oil in the frying pan with the garlic. Brown the meat. Remove to a casserole dish. Brown the parsnips and onions in the frying pan. Remove and discard the garlic. Stir in the stock, soy sauce, golden syrup, vinegar and grated ginger. Bring to the boil and pour over meat. Cover the casserole.

Ensure the casserole is piping hot, then transfer to the top oven set at "Simmer" (150C/300F) for 2 hours.

Mix the cornflour with a little water. Stir into the casserole and heat on the simmering end of the hot plate or, if the casserole dish is not flameproof return it to the oven, until the sauce has thickened. Adjust seasoning and serve.

Serves 4-6.

MAIN COURSE

CHICKEN AND PRUNE CASSEROLE

This makes a rich chicken dish, easy to make. I find it a good recipe for cold winter days.

6-8 chicken portions
4 garlic cloves
2 level tsp dried mixed herbs
2 tbsp red wine vinegar
4 fl oz/100ml oil
8 oz/225g pitted, ready to eat prunes
salt and pepper
1/2 pint/300ml dry white wine
1 oz/25g demerara sugar
1 level tsp cornflour
1/4 pint/150 ml chicken stock

Place the chicken in a large, non-metallic bowl. Add sliced garlic cloves, mixed herbs, wine vinegar, oil, prunes and seasoning and mix well. Cover well and marinate in the fridge overnight.

Remove the chicken from the marinade and fry it until golden brown in a little oil skimmed from the marinade. Transfer to a flameproof casserole dish. Add the marinade mixture and the wine. Sprinkle in the sugar.

Bring to the boil on the hot plate, boil for 2-3 minutes, cover and place in the middle of the top oven set at "Bake" (200C/400F) for 45 minutes.

Blend the cornflour and chicken stock. Remove the casserole from the oven. Serve the chicken onto a plate, keep warm in the bottom oven. Add the stock mixture to the marinade, heat it on the simmering end of the hot plate stirring until thickened. Pour the sauce over the chicken.

Garnish with chopped parsley and serve.

Serves 6-8.

HERB BAKED CHICKEN

I love to make this in the summer when there are plenty of fresh herbs to add flavour to plain chicken. I add a bunch of mixed fresh herbs to the bread in the food processor and everything is then chopped together. The amount of herbs used depends upon taste.

4 chicken portions – skinless
1 egg
seasoned flour
6 oz/175g white/brown breadcrumbs
1 tbsp finely chopped parsley
2 tbsp finely chopped mixed herbs or 2 tsp dried mixed herbs
salt and pepper
grated rind of ¹/₂ a lemon
2 oz/50g butter

Beat the egg in a shallow dish. Spoon a little seasoned flour onto a plate.

Measure the breadcrumbs into a basin, stir in parsley, herbs, salt, pepper and lemon rind. Melt the butter – stand on the Rayburn in a basin, stir into the crumbs and fork well.

Roll the chicken portions first in the flour, then in the egg and finally in the breadcrumbs, patting them on firmly. Place the chicken portions in the small roasting tin, and slide it onto the third set of runners from the top of the top oven set at "Roast" (250C/475F) and bake for 30-40 minutes until crisp, golden and cooked through – there should be no pink juices when pierced with a sharp knife.

Serve with a good green salad and crusty bread.

Serves 4.

CHICKEN IN RED WINE WITH RAISINS

....

The sauce for this casserole dish is rich and spicy and makes a lovely winter dish. During cooking the raisins and apricots become plump and juicy.

1/2 pint/300ml red wine
3 tbsp red wine vinegar
2 oz/50g seedless raisins
4 oz/100g no-soak dried apricots – halved
1 tsp ground ginger
1 tsp ground cinnamon
1/2 inch/1cm piece fresh root ginger – peeled and grated
4 cloves
4 juniper berries – lightly crushed
4 chicken portions
2 tbsp flour
salt and pepper
knob of butter
1 tbsp vegetable oil
1/2 pint/300ml chicken stock

Put the wine, vinegar, raisins, apricots, ground ginger, cinnamon, fresh ginger, cloves and juniper berries in a non-metallic dish. Add the chicken pieces and cover with the marinade. Cover and leave to marinate for at least 3-4 hours or overnight.

Remove the chicken from the marinade and pat dry on kitchen paper. Season the flour with salt and pepper and then coat the chicken with the flour. Heat the oil and butter in a flameproof casserole dish, add the chicken, skin side down, and fry until golden brown. Turn and brown the other side. Lift the chicken out and put to one side. Pour off any excess fat. Pour the marinade and stock into the casserole dish, bring to the boil, stirring, return the chicken. Boil for 2-3 minutes and then transfer, covered, to the middle of the top oven set at "Simmer" (150C/300F) for 1-1½ hours until the chicken is tender. Transfer the chicken to a warm plate. Boil the liquid to reduce to a thicker sauce. Pour over the chicken. Lovely with boiled rice.

Serves 4.

....

TURKEY BURGERS

....

Homemade burgers are much nicer than anything bought in the shops. They are quick and easy to make, either by hand or in a processor. Turkey meat is low in fat and healthy, but it does need some flavouring. Cook these in the oven and serve with home-made oven chips (*see page 82*).

1 small onion – finely chopped
1 lb/450g minced turkey
2 oz/50g fresh breadcrumbs or porridge oats
grated rind of ¹/₂ a small lemon
2 tbsp chopped parsley
8 streaky bacon rashers – rind off
salt and pepper
a little oil

If making by hand, fry the onion in a little oil until soft, then combine with the minced turkey meat, breadcrumbs, lemon rind, parsley and salt and pepper to taste. Alternatively put the onion in the processor and chop finely. Add all the ingredients except the bacon and process them together.

Shape into eight burgers. Cut each rasher in half lengthways, and wrap two rashers round each burger in a cross formation. Place the burgers on a baking tray and drizzle a little oil over them. Put the tray of burgers on the floor of the top oven set at "Roast" (230C/450F) for 15 minutes, then put the top shelf on the top set of runners in the top oven and move the tray of burgers up for 10-15 minutes to give a crisp finish to the bacon.

Makes 8 burgers.
....

STIR-FRY

Many people think they cannot stir-fry on their Rayburn. I find it very successful using the hottest part of the hot plate and a large frying pan. This recipe can be adapted for vegetarians and meat eaters alike. Tofu, a bean curd, has little flavour of its own, so it is a good idea to marinate before cooking. The same can be said of turkey or chicken strips, so treat in the same way.

2 tbsp soy sauce
2 tbsp dry sherry
2 tbsp orange juice
2 spring onions – sliced
1 clove garlic – crushed
8 oz/225g tofu- cubed or 12 oz/350g chicken or turkey stir-fry strips
2 tbsp sesame oil
1 oz/25g flaked almonds
1 red pepper – cored, de-seeded and sliced
6 oz/175g mange-tout, topped, tailed and halved
4 oz/100g button mushrooms – sliced
8 oz/225g bean sprouts
2 tbsp sesame seeds, toasted (place on a baking tray in the top of the roasting oven for 2-5 minutes – watch them as they burn easily)

Mix the soy sauce, sherry, orange juice, onion and garlic in a basin. Toss in either the tofu or the meat strips. Cover and leave to marinate for 1 hour. Heat the oil in a large frying pan, add the almonds, fry for 1 minute to brown on all sides, remove with slotted spoon to a plate, and then keep warm in the lower oven. Add the tofu cubes or meat slices to the hot pan and stir-fry until beginning to brown. 2-3 minutes for the tofu, 5 minutes for the meat. Remove them to the plate in the lower oven.

Add the peppers and mange-tout, stir-fry for about 2 minutes, stir in the mushrooms and beansprouts, cook for 1 minute. Add the almonds and the marinade, cook for 2 minutes, stir in the tofu or meat, heat through and serve, sprinkled with the sesame seeds.

Serves 4.

LIVER STROGANOFF

....

This is a quick and easy dish, tasty enough to serve to guests and liked by those uncertain about eating liver. It is nothing like the well-cooked liver of school days! Hot ribbon noodles, such as tagliatelle, go well.

¹/₂ oz/12g butter
1 medium onion – skinned and sliced
1 lb/450g lamb's liver – cut into strips
1 tbsp flour
4 oz/100g button mushrooms
¹/₄ pint/150ml stock
4 tomatoes – skinned and roughly chopped
1 tbsp Worcestershire sauce
salt and pepper
5 fl oz soured cream or thick yogurt

Melt the butter in a large frying pan and gently fry the onion until soft and cooked.

Put the liver, salt and pepper and flour in a plastic bag. Shake to coat the liver in flour. Add the liver to the pan along with the mushrooms. Fry for 5 minutes, stirring well. Add the stock and bring to the boil.

Stir in the tomatoes and Worcestershire sauce. Simmer for 3-4 minutes. Stir in the cream and reheat without boiling. Serve.

Serves 4.
....

SAUSAGE PAPRIKA

....

This is a wonderful way to cook sausages. Everything is cooked in one dish in the oven. Just serve with baked potatoes for a warming, economical dish.

1 lb/450g herb sausages
1 tbsp oil
2 large onions – chopped
4 oz/100g mushrooms – sliced
15 oz/425g can chopped tomatoes
2 tbsp tomato purée
2 tsp paprika
salt
5 oz/150g carton plain yoghurt
chopped parsley to garnish

Lay sausages in a single layer in an ovenproof dish. Put the oven shelf on the second set of runners from the top in the top oven set at "Bake" (180C/350F), put in the sausages and brown them for about 5-10 minutes.

Remove sausages from the dish to a plate in the lower oven to keep warm. Pour oil into the ovenproof dish and put on the floor of the top oven, heat for 1-2 minutes. Stir in the onions and cook for 10 minutes, stirring occasionally. Add the mushrooms, stir and cook for 4-5 minutes. Stir in the tomatoes, purée, paprika and a pinch of salt. Return the sausages to the dish, and cover with a lid or foil. Put the shelf on the bottom set of runners, put in the sausage dish for 30-40 minutes.

Stir in the yoghurt, return to oven to heat through. Sprinkle with chopped parsley.

Serve with baked potatoes.

Serves 4.

....

VENISON CASSEROLE

....

Venison is now readily available in supermarkets and makes a richly flavoured casserole. This is an ideal traditional Rayburn dish, cooked gently in a low oven to give tender meat and a delicious flavour.

1¹/₂ lb/675g casserole venison – diced
2 onions – peeled and sliced
1 clove garlic – peeled and crushed
2 tbsp flour
2 tbsp oil
salt and pepper
¹/₄ pint/150ml stock
¹/₂ pint/300ml red wine
1 tbsp sage – chopped or 1 tsp dried sage
4 oz/100g button mushrooms

Season the flour with the salt and pepper, then toss the diced meat in it.

Heat the oil in a flameproof casserole and cook the onions gently until softened. Stir in the meat and cook until browned. Stir in the garlic, stock, wine and sage. Bring to the boil, cover and transfer to the top oven set at "Simmer" (1250C/300F) for 2-3 hours until the meat is tender.

Stir in the mushrooms and return to the oven for a further 15-20 minutes. Serve with creamy, mashed potatoes.

Serves 4-6.
....

ROAST DUCK WITH GREEN PEAS

Duckling is less fatty now, but can still produce a lot of fat during the cooking process, so cooking this in the roasting tin with the grill rack makes for a moist but not fatty meat.

1 oven-ready duckling, about 4¹/₂ lbs/2kg in weight
salt and pepper
16 (approx) small onions or shallots – skinned
2 oz/50g streaky bacon rashers – rinded and diced
1 lb/450g frozen peas
4 tbsp chicken stock or white wine

Weigh the duckling, prick the skin all over and rub with salt. Stand it on the high setting of the rack in the roasting tin. Place a loose cover of foil over. Roast on the bottom set of runners of the top oven set to "Roast" (200C/400F) for 30 minutes per 1 lb/450g.

Half an hour before the end of the cooking time, remove the duckling and rack, and drain off most of the fat from the roasting tin. Stand the roasting tin on the simmering end of the hot plate and brown the onions in the hot fat. Add the bacon and stir for 2-3 minutes until the fat runs. Mix the peas into the onion mixture with some salt and pepper. Stir in the stock or wine. Return the duckling, on the rack, to the roasting tin and return to the oven, uncovered. Cook for a further 30 minutes.

Serve on a warm platter, surrounded by the vegetables.

Serves 4.

PIGEON AND PLUM CASSEROLE

Pigeons and plums are in season together and combine in this casserole to make a slightly sweet and sour mixture. The cooking time for the pigeons will depend on how young and tender the pigeons are.

1 oz/25g butter
1 tbsp vegetable oil
4 pigeons – dressed
2 tsp flour
1 medium onion – skinned and chopped
2 cloves
1 bouquet garni
¹/₄ pint/150ml port
1 lb/450g plums – stoned and halved
salt and pepper
a little grated nutmeg

Heat the butter and oil in a flameproof casserole. Coat the pigeons in the flour and then fry them until browned on all sides. Remove them to a warm plate.

Fry the onion in the casserole until softening, return the pigeons to the pan and add the bouquet garni, cloves and port. Arrange the plums over the top. Cover with a tightly fitting lid. Bring to the boil and then transfer to the top oven set at "Simmer" (150C/300F) for about 2 hours, until the pigeons are tender.

Transfer the pigeons and plums to a serving plate. Boil the juices to thicken, season with salt, pepper and nutmeg and pour over the pigeon.

Serves 4.

PIZZA

....

I use a standard bread dough enriched with some olive oil for my pizzas. Some freshly chopped herbs or a teaspoon of dried herbs can also be added. You can of course also use a packet of pizza base mix. A variety of toppings can be used, but a good tomato base is always needed. In winter I make a topping using canned tomatoes, but in summer, when tomatoes have more flavour and are more plentiful, I spread the base with chopped tomatoes and then put on my toppings.

TOMATO SAUCE
1 tbsp olive oil
1 onion, finely chopped
1 clove garlic, peeled and crushed
¹/₂ tsp dried basil
1 tbsp tomato purée
1 x 14 oz/400g chopped tomatoes – drained
salt and pepper

Heat the oil in a saucepan, stir in the chopped onions and the garlic and cook until softened.

Stir in the remaining ingredients, bring to the boil, cover and transfer to the top oven set at "Simmer" (150C/300F) for half an hour.

Spread over the pizza bases, leaving ¹/₄ inch/5mm border all round. Finish with a selection of toppings.

PIZZA BASE
1 lb/450g bread flour
1 tsp salt
1 tsp herbs
1 sachet of easy-blend yeast
4 tbsp olive oil
¹/₂ pint/300ml warm water, approximately

Measure flour into a mixing bowl. Stir in salt and yeast. Stir in olive oil and herbs if using. Blend in the warm water – enough to make a manageable dough for kneading.

Knead the dough on a floured worktop for at least 5 minutes until pliable. Divide the dough into 2 and roll to 10 inch/25cm rounds.

I like my pizzas to have a very crispy base so I brush the pizza with oil and turn it over onto a baking sheet. If you prefer, you may just place them, slightly floury, on a baking tray.

Place a folded tea-towel on top of the Rayburn and stand the pizza base tray on top to rise for about 30 minutes.

Meanwhile prepare the topping.

Makes 2 large pizzas.

....

A FEW TOPPING SUGGESTIONS
• *Chopped black olives, red pepper slices and crumbled feta cheese.*
• *Just lashings of grated Swiss Gruyère.*
• *Salami slices, chopped black olives and Mozzarella cheese grated.*
• *Thinly sliced streaky bacon and finely sliced mushrooms.*
• *Slices of finely sliced ham and pineapple pieces.*

BAKING THE PIZZA
When the base is risen and fluffy and the toppings are finished slide the pizza tray onto the floor of the top oven heated to "Bake" (200C/400F) for 15 minutes – this will ensure a crisp base. Have the oven shelf on the second set of runners from the top and after 15 minutes transfer the pizza to the shelf for a further 10-15 minutes to cook the topping.

VEGETABLES AND VEGETARIAN

WENSLEYDALE AND WATERCRESS TART

This recipe gives the quantity for the tart to be made in the roasting tin, which is useful if you are catering for a crowd. The filling can be altered but the basic quantity of eggs and milk or cream are given.

1 1/2 lb/700g shortcrust pastry
9 eggs
1 pint/600ml single cream
1/2 pint/300ml milk
salt and pepper
2 bunches watercress – washed and finely chopped
grated fresh nutmeg
12 oz/350g Wensleydale – crumbled or grated

Using the shortcrust pastry, line the roasting tin. Beat together the eggs, cream, milk, salt and pepper. Stir in the chopped watercress and nutmeg. Add the cheese. Pour the mixture into the prepared pastry case. Put the roasting tin on the floor of the top oven set at "Bake" (200C/400F) and bake for 40-50 minutes until the filling is set.

VARIATIONS:

Replace the cream with milk. Leave out the watercress, nutmeg and Wensleydale and use a selection of the following:

1 lb/450g streaky bacon – fried
3 chopped onions – sauteed
12 oz/350g grated cheese
1 lb/450g spinach – cooked and chopped

Serves 12-14.

SOUFFLES

Soufflés are so easy to make, but the crucial point comes at serving time. Make this when it can be guaranteed that everyone will be ready to eat as soon as the soufflé is cooked. The Rayburn is ideal for soufflés because the oven is hot, so you get a well risen soufflé that remains beautifully moist inside. This is a basic cheese soufflé recipe, but I have given a list of variations at the end.

2 oz/50g butter
2 oz/50g butter
¹/₂ pint/300ml milk
4 oz/100g grated Gruyère
pinch grated nutmeg
salt and pepper
3 egg yolks and 4 egg whites

Melt the butter in a saucepan, stir in the flour and cook for 1 minute. Gradually stir in the milk until a thick sauce forms, boil for 3 minutes beating well to make the sauce thick and glossy. Remove from the heat, beat in the cheese, a little salt, pepper, nutmeg and the egg yolks.

Whisk the egg whites until stiff.Fold 1 tablespoon egg white into the sauce. Gently fold the sauce into the remaining egg whites using a metal spoon. Gently pour into a well buttered 2¹/₂ pint (1.5l) soufflé dish. Heat the top oven to "Bake" (180C/350F), put the shelf on the bottom set of runners and slide in the soufflé dish. Bake for 25-30 minutes until the soufflé is risen with a high golden crown. Serve at once.

VARIATIONS
Replace the cheese with one of the following:

* *4 oz/100g finely chopped ham*
* *4oz/100g finely flaked smoked mackerel*
* *4 oz/100g finely chopped, fried mushrooms*
* *8 oz/200g cooked finely chopped spinach, and 2 oz/100g grated Gruyère and a pinch of nutmeg.*

Serves 4.

PASTA WITH ASPARAGUS AND PARMESAN

....

1 onion – finely chopped
14 oz/400g thin asparagus
2 oz/50g butter
3 fl oz/90ml dry white wine
14 oz/400g dried pasta shapes (penne or spirals)
10 fl oz/284ml extra thick double cream
salt and pepper
2 oz/50g Parmesan cheese – grated

Cut the asparagus into 2 inch/5cm lengths, and blanch them in boiling water for 2-3 minutes until tender. Reserve 5 tablespoons of the blanching liquid.

Melt the butter in a saucepan on the simmering end of the hot plate. Cook the onion until soft. Add the asparagus, pour in the reserved blanching liquid and the wine. Cook until most of the liquid has evaporated.

Cook the pasta on the hottest part of the plate in plenty of boiling, salted water until *al dente*. Drain.

Add the cream to the sauce and stir well. Heat gently until bubbling. Stir in half the cheese, taste and season.

Toss the sauce into the pasta. Serve with the remaining Parmesan sprinkled over.

Serves 4-6.
....

JACKET OR BAKED POTATOES

Jacket potatoes baked in the Rayburn bear no resemblance to potatoes baked in the microwave oven or even in some gas and electric ovens. They have a crisp "jacket" and a fluffy middle. Choose maincrop potatoes, of an even size so that they cook evenly together. The fluffiness of the inside will depend upon the variety chosen. Scrub the potatoes well. Cut a cross in the middle to slit the skin and prevent bursting. I find that at the end of the cooking the potato can be squeezed on the bottom and the cross opens up. This is lovely with a knob of butter or a dollop of soured cream. The potatoes can also be scooped out after baking, the inside forked together with a variety of fillings and returned to the shell. Heat through again. Serve with salad for a complete meal.

To bake the potatoes: place the prepared potatoes directly on the oven shelf. Have the shelf on the third set of runners from the top in the top oven set at "Roast" (230C/450F) for approximately 1 hour – this time will vary according to the size of the potatoes chosen.

FILLING IDEAS:
- *grated cheese*
- *cottage cheese*
- *diced ham,*
- *crispy diced bacon*
- *tuna fish and mayonnaise,*
- *sweetcorn and chives*
- *beaten egg and cheese.*

OVEN CHIPS

··

These are a cross between baked potatoes and shop-bought oven chips. They have a good flavour and can be as crispy as you like.

1 lb/450g maincrop potatoes – scrubbed
1 tbsp olive oil
salt

Heat the oil in the roasting tin.

Slice the potatoes into fingers, about eight for each potato, and toss in the oil. Sprinkle on a little salt.

Hang the tin from the top set of runners in the top oven set at "Roast" (230C/450F). Cook for half an hour. Stir round to re-coat with the oil. Cook for a further 20-30 minutes – move the tin down oven if they are browning too much.

The cooking time will vary according to the type of potato used.

Serve with turkey burgers, grilled meat or fish. Sprinkle with sea salt before serving.

Serves 4.
··

ROSTI

....

This is a typical Swiss dish that I find a popular way to serve potatoes. Serve with thin slices of Emmental or Gruyère and a side salad for a complete meal.

2¹/₂ lb/1125g waxy potatoes
salt and pepper
2 oz/50g butter
2 tbsp oil

Wash the potatoes. Try to have the potatoes roughly the same size so that they cook evenly.

Place the potatoes in a saucepan of boiling water. Cover and move to the top oven set at "Simmer" (150C/300F) for 20-30 minutes until the potatoes are just tender – this will depend on the size of the potatoes and the type. Drain and put to one side to cool. This can be done the day before they are needed.

Peel and coarsely grate the potatoes, seasoning with salt and pepper.

Heat half the butter and oil in a heavy frying pan, move to the hottest part of the hot plate and press the potatoes in to make a cake.

Cook for 10-15 minutes, transferring to the cooler end if too hot, until the bottom is golden and crusty.

Invert the rösti onto a plate. Heat the rest of the butter and oil in the pan, slide the rösti back into the pan and cook the second side for about 10 minutes.

Serve hot cut into wedges.

Serves 4.
....

ROAST MEDITERRANEAN VEGETABLES

....

I find this a quick and easy method of cooking vegetables like aubergines and courgettes, and it really brings out their fresh flavour. Serve them hot or cold tossed in French dressing or even layer them up, after cooking, to make a vegetarian lasagne. Add tomatoes, roughly chopped, for the last 10 minutes to make a ratatouille mixture.

A SELECTION TO SUIT THE SEASON OR YOUR TASTE:

- *aubergine*
- *courgette*
- *red pepper*
- *yellow pepper*
- *shallots*
- *olive oil*
- *sea salt*

Dice the vegetables into roughly 1 inch cubes. Place in the roasting tin. Toss in 1-2 tablespoons of olive oil, just to coat. The amount of oil will vary according to the amount of vegetables. Toss with a little sea salt.

Slide the roasting tin onto the top set of runners of the top oven set at "Bake" (220C/425F).

Roast the vegetables for 20-30 minutes until cooked but still firm.

CRUMBED TOMATOES

....

This is a good winter vegetable standby to serve with chops instead of a sauce.

2 medium onions
2 oz/50g butter
2 x 14 oz/400g cans tomatoes
6 oz/175g breadcrumbs
1 tsp chopped parsley
finely grated rind of ¹/₂ a lemon
salt and pepper

Peel and finely slice the onions. Melt 1 oz/25g butter in a pan and stir in the onions. Cook slowly until golden brown. Spoon into a shallow, oven-proof dish.

Halve or quarter the tomatoes and pour over the onions, with the tomato juice.

Mix the breadcrumbs with the parsley, lemon rind, salt and pepper and scatter over the tomatoes. Dot with shavings of the remaining 1 oz/25g butter.

Bake in the middle of the top oven set at "Bake" (220C/425F) for 30 minutes until bubbling hot and crisp on top.

Serves 4-6.

....

PEPPERONATA

....

This is the most tasty way I know of cooking peppers and it looks most attractive. Cut the peppers and tomatoes to similar shapes and sizes to make the finished dish look its best.

6 small peppers, assorted colours
4 tbsp olive oil
2 onions, skinned and finely sliced
1 clove garlic, skinned and crushed
1 lb/450g plum tomatoes, skinned, quartered and seeded
2 tbsp balsamic vinegar
10-12 black olives, pitted and halved
salt and pepper

Wash, quarter and seed the peppers.

Heat the oil in a large cast iron pan on the hot plate. Stir in the onions and cook for about 5 minutes until soft. Add the garlic and peppers, stir occasionally and cook for 10-15 minutes until the peppers are softening.

Stir in the tomatoes and cook again for 5-10 more minutes. Stir in the vinegar, salt and pepper and olives.

This method can be carried out with the pan on the floor of the top oven if there is room when the oven is hot.

Serve hot or cold.

This will serve 8 as a starter with crusty bread or 4-6 as an accompaniment.
....

STUFFED TOMATOES

....

These tomatoes make a good starter for eight or a light lunch for four. The baking seems to bring out the sweet flavour of the tomatoes. Prepare in advance and bake when needed.

4 large beefsteak tomatoes
salt and pepper
3 tbsp parsley – chopped
2 tbsp basil – chopped
6 tbsp grated Sbrinz or Parmesan
6 tbsp fresh breadcrumbs
1 tbsp olive oil

Cut the tomatoes in half horizontally. Scoop out most of the insides, using a sharp teaspoon or grapefruit knife.

Mix together the parsley, basil, 4 tablespoons of grated cheese, salt and pepper and breadcrumbs. Fill the tomatoes with the stuffing. Stand in a lightly oiled oven-proof dish.

Put the oven shelf in the middle of the top oven set at "Bake" (180C/360F). Put in the tomatoes and bake for 20 minutes or until golden brown and the tomatoes are softened.

Sprinkle on the remaining cheese and serve with warm crusty bread.

Serves 4 for lunch or 8 for starters.
....

MUSHROOM RISOTTO

....

This is a delicious dish for anyone who loves mushrooms. 4 oz/100g crisply cooked bacon can be added at the end if you are not cooking for a vegetarian. Dried porcini mushrooms can be soaked in water for half an hour and used if fresh varieties are not available. Use the soaking liquid for cooking the risotto.

4 oz/100g assorted wild mushrooms – sliced
1 medium onion – chopped
2 tbsp olive oil
2 oz/50g butter
1 clove garlic – finely chopped
1-1½ pints/600-900ml light stock – hot
10 oz/275g risotto rice
8 tbsp white wine
2 oz/50g finely grated Sbrinz or Parmesan cheese

Fry the onion in the oil and half the butter in a deep frying pan on the simmering end of the hot plate until soft and pale gold. Stir in the garlic and the mushrooms.

Stir in the rice until well coated with the butter, add the wine and boil for about 2 minutes until it is absorbed. Gradually add the stock, stirring, until it is all absorbed and the rice is cooked, about 10-15 minutes. The rice should not become soggy and should have a little sauce round it – you may not need all the stock.

Remove from the heat, stir in the butter and most of the cheese. Taste and season. Serve with remaining grated cheese.

Serves 4.
....

MIXED RICE PILAFF

Wild rice is expensive, but a small amount mixed with brown rice will add flavour and texture as well as enhance the appearance. Serve this pilaff with casserole.

12 oz/350g long-grain brown rice
2 oz/50g wild rice
4 tbsp olive oil
salt and pepper
2 oz/50g pine kernels – toasted

Measure the washed rice into a saucepan, add 1½ times as much water and a good pinch of salt. Bring to the boil on the hot plate. Cover with a lid and transfer to the top oven set at "Simmer" (150C/300F). Cook for about 20 minutes, until the rice is cooked and most of the water absorbed. Drain well.

Stir the oil into the drained, warm rice. Stir in the toasted pine kernels and adjust seasoning.

Serves 6.

MIXED VEGETABLE RING

....

This recipe came about because I needed a quick vegetarian supper dish. Choux pastry baked in the Rayburn is deliciously puffy and moist. I have also used this recipe with 4 oz/100g prawns stirred in for non-vegetarians.

RING

Follow the recipe as for Gougère (see page 35) to end of the third paragraph.

Grease a baking tray. Spoon out tablespoons of the mixture into a circle. Bake in the top oven set at "Bake" (220C/425F) with the shelf on the third set of runners from the top. Check after 15 minutes, if browning move down with the shelf on the floor of the oven. Bake for a further 20-30 minutes until risen, puffy and golden brown.

FILLING
1 oz/25g butter
1 large onion – chopped
1 clove garlic – crushed
2 oz/50g mushrooms – sliced
2 courgettes – finely sliced
1 small aubergine – diced
1 red pepper – seeded and sliced
3 tomatoes – skinned and chopped
salt and pepper

Melt the butter in a saucepan, stir in the onion and cook until softened. Stir in remaining ingredients, and cover with a lid. Bring to simmering point on the cooler end of the hot plate. Cook gently for about 20-30 minutes until the vegetables are cooked by not mushy.

Place the choux ring on a large oven-proof plate and spoon the vegetable filling into the centre. If liked, pop into the roasting oven for 5-10 minutes until piping hot.

Serve immediately with a side salad and crusty bread.

Serves 4.
....

BROCCOLI QUICHE

I found this recipe persuaded my children to eat green vegetables because of the thin layer of tomato ketchup in the base!

8 oz/225g shortcrust pastry
8 oz/225g Broccoli – broken into florets
2 tbsp tomato ketchup
3 eggs
¹/₂ pint/300ml milk
salt and pepper
4 oz/100g grated Gruyère

Line a 9 inch/23cm flan dish with the shortcrust pastry. Cook the broccoli in a small amount of boiling, salted water until crisp and still bright green. Drain.

Spread the ketchup over the base of the pastry case. Lay on the drained Broccoli florets over the ketchup.

Beat together the eggs, milk, salt and pepper and half the grated cheese. and pour over the broccoli. Sprinkle over the remaining cheese. Bake on the floor of the top oven set at "Bake" (220C/300F) for about 30 minutes until golden brown and set.

Serves 6.

COURGETTE TART

....

This is a good way to use up courgettes in the summer and a good vegetarian dish.

¹/₂ lb/225g shortcrust pastry
1 onion – chopped
2 tbsp olive oil
4-6 small courgettes – finely sliced
salt and pepper
4 eggs
¹/₂ pint/300ml single cream
¹/₄ pint/150ml milk
freshly grated nutmeg
4 oz/100g Gruyère – grated

Roll out the pastry to line a 9 or 10 inch/23 or 25cm flan dish. Fry the onion gently in the olive oil until soft. Remove with a slotted spoon to the pastry case.

Fry the courgettes until golden brown. Remove to the pastry case.

Beat the eggs, add the milk, cream, salt and pepper and the nutmeg. Pour this mixture over the courgettes and sprinkle over the grated Gruyère.

Bake on the floor of the top oven set at "Bake" (220C/425F) for about 30 minutes until the tart is set in the middle and golden brown.

Serves 6.
....

BEAN AND TOMATO CASSEROLE

....

This is a filling dish, lovely on its own with green salad.

3 oz/75g red kidney beans
3 oz/75g black-eyed beans
3 oz/75g butter beans
1 large onion – chopped
2 sticks celery – chopped
2 tbsp oil
1 clove garlic – crushed
14 oz/400g can tomatoes – chopped
1/4 pint/150ml light stock
1/4 tsp chilli powder
salt and pepper
3 oz/75g wholemeal breadcrumbs
4 oz/100g tasty cheese – grated

Soak the beans in water overnight. Drain and place them in a large saucepan. Cover with water, bring to the boil and boil rapidly for 10-15 minutes. Cover and transfer to the top oven set at "Simmer" (150C/300F) for about 1 hour, until all the beans are cooked. Drain and rinse.

Heat the oil in a pan and cook the onion and celery until they begin to soften. Add the garlic and fry until soft. Stir in the tomatoes and stock, chilli powder, beans, salt and pepper to taste. Bring to the boil, cover and return to the bottom shelf of the oven for 30-40 minutes. Transfer to an ovenproof dish. Mix the breadcrumbs and cheese and scatter over the bean mixture. Place towards the top of the oven for 10-15 minutes until golden brown and crusty.

Serves 4.
....

L E N T I L   R I S S O L E S

These tasty rissoles are a good introduction to lentils for anyone who is a devoted meat eater. Serve with home-made tomato sauce.

2 tbsp oil
1 onion – finely chopped
2 carrots – finely diced
8 oz/225g orange lentils – washed and picked over
1 pint/600ml water
1 tsp ground coriander
2 tbsp parsley – chopped
6 oz/175g wholemeal breadcrumbs
2 tbsp flour
1 egg – beaten
salt and pepper

Heat the oil in a saucepan, add the onion, celery and carrot and cook until softened. Stir in the lentils, water, coriander and salt and pepper. Bring to the boil, cover and transfer to the top oven set at "Simmer" (150C/300F) for 1-1¹/₂ hours until the lentils are cooked and the liquid has been absorbed.

Mix in the parsley and 2 oz/50g breadcrumbs. Turn the mixture onto a plate and allow to cool for a little.

Using floured hands shape the mixture into rissoles or cakes. Dip in the beaten egg and then the remaining breadcrumbs.

Heat a little oil in a frying pan on the hot plate and fry the rissoles until crisp and golden on both sides.

Makes 8 rissoles.

YORKSHIRE PUDDINGS

A Yorkshire pudding is neither a vegetable nor a vegetarian meal, yet it finds itself in this section, unwanted by any other, but wonderful nevertheless. Yorkshire puddings need a good, hot oven to make them puff up, so to overcome the problem of slightly low heat at the end of the roast cooking time, I cook my Yorkshire puddings before the meat goes in the oven! Yes, it does work. Cook the puddings in the usual way. When fully cooked, remove them and put them to one side. When the joint is removed for resting before carving, return the pudding to the roasting oven to heat through.

4 oz/100g plain flour
pinch salt
1 egg
¹/₂ pint/300ml milk
a little lard or dripping

Sieve the flour and salt into a basin. Make a well in the centre and crack in the egg. Beat the egg with a wooden spoon, gradually drawing in the flour. Slowly add the milk, beating the batter well until a smooth, creamy batter has been made.

Place a little lard or dripping into the base of 8 little bun tins.

Set the top oven to "Roast" (220C/425F) and put the oven shelf on the third set of runners from the top. Put in the tray to get hot. Leave until the fat is melted and hazy hot.

Remove from the oven and pour in the batter. Return to the oven and cook until risen and crisp and golden brown, about 25-30 minutes.

Makes 8 bun-size puddings.

PUDDINGS

CREME CARAMEL

....

This ever popular dish can be served as a light dessert, made in advance to allow chilling and for the flavours to develop. This recipe serves six, either made in one soufflé dish, or in individual ramekin dishes.

CARAMEL
4 oz/100g granulated sugar
3 tbsp water

CUSTARD
4 eggs
1 pint/600ml milk
3 oz/75g caster sugar
a few drops of vanilla essence

Put the sugar for the caramel in a clean, dry saucepan. If you are making individual ramekins you may like to use an ounce or two more of sugar. Stand the pan on the simmering end of the hot plate and heat gently to dissolve the sugar, heating until it turns to a caramel colour. Keep an eye on it! Remove from the heat and stir in the water to stop the caramel cooking further – but take care, it may spatter your hand. Return the pan to the simmering plate and stir until a thick caramel sauce is formed. Pour the sauce into the dish or ramekins.

Lightly whisk the eggs, add the vanilla essence. Pour the milk and sugar into a saucepan and heat gently on the simmering plate just until the sugar is dissolved. Pour onto the eggs and beat well. Strain the mixture through a sieve into a jug. Pour over the prepared caramel.

Stand the dish or ramekins in the roasting tin. Pour boiling water around the dishes to come about half way up the sides of the roasting tin. Cover with a sheet of foil.

Slide the tin onto the bottom set of runners in the top oven set on "Simmer" (100C/200F) for 1^1/$_2$ hours or until the custard is completely set. Leave to cool and chill before turning out.

Serves 6.
....

STEAMED PUDDINGS

Steamed puddings are marvellous when cooked in the Rayburn, and the kitchen does not fill with steam. I am giving the recipe for a fairly basic steamed pudding and several variations, you may of course want to try your own. These old-fashioned puddings are becoming popular again because of their flavour and though, with modern eating trends, we will not revert to this sort of pudding daily it is great for a treat. I find a steamed pudding good for a supper party because it can be left cooking slowly in a low temperature oven, even if guests are late or we are lingering over the main course.

6 oz/175g self raising flour
pinch salt
4 oz/100g butter or soft margarine
4 oz/100g caster sugar
2 eggs

Grease well a 2 pint/1.1 litre pudding basin. The plastic boilable ones with a lid are useful. Spoon your topping choice into the bottom of the basin.

Beat together the flour, salt, butter, sugar and eggs to a soft consistency. If it is very dry, especially with wholemeal flour, beat in a little milk. Carefully put into the prepared basin.

Cover with a circle of greaseproof paper and either a sheet of pleated foil or the plastic lid.

Use a deep enough saucepan to take the pudding basin standing on a trivet, or an old saucer or a wad of newspaper. Stand the pudding in the pan on the trivet. Pour in enough boiling water to come half way up the basin. Cover. Stand the pan on the simmering end of the hot plate, bring to the boil and simmer (if necessary move slightly off the plate) for 30 minutes. Remove to the top oven set on "Simmer" (150C/300F) for about 2 hours. The pudding will continue to steam – the water should not need topping up. Turn out onto a warm plate and serve with cream, yoghurt, custard or more topping sauce.

Serves 6.

VARIATION

CHOCOLATE AND BRAZIL NUT

3 tbsp cocoa
2 oz/50g brazil nuts

Add 3 tbsp cocoa, sifted with the flour, to the basic mixture. Chop the nuts and fold into the mixture before putting in the basin.

TOPPINGS

1. STICKY TOFFEE PUDDING

7 oz/200g soft brown sugar
4 oz/100g butter
6 tbsp double cream

Place all the ingredients in a small saucepan. stir over gentle heat to melt the butter and dissolve the sugar. Bring to the boil and simmer for 3 minutes. Pour into the basin before adding the sponge mixture.

2. MARMALADE

3 tbsp marmalade

Put the marmalade into the bottom of the basin.

3. SYRUP

3 tbsp golden syrup

Put the warmed syrup into the bottom of the basin.

PAVLOVA

....

This is always a popular dessert for a special meal. I make my meringues dry so that they can be made in advance and stored – either in a box in the freezer or a dry cupboard. I can also fill them an hour or two before serving, which allows time for the cream and filling to soften the meringue slightly and me time to get on with other preparations!

3 egg whites
6 oz/175g caster sugar or 4 oz/100g caster sugar and
2 oz/50g soft brown sugar
1 tsp white wine vinegar and 1 tsp cornflour blended together

Prepare a baking sheet, line with non-stick parchment or a re-usable non-stick baking sheet. Whisk the egg whites in a clean, dry and grease-free bowl until white and fluffy. Continue to whisk, adding the sugar 1 teaspoonful at a time. When all the sugar is in, whisk in the cornflour mixture.

Using tablespoons, spoon the meringue into a circle. Use some meringue to fill in the circle but ensure the sides are higher than the base. Roughen the edges. Bake in the top oven set on its lowest or idling setting on the bottom set of runners for two hours. If the meringues are not dry enough either return to this low temperature oven or place in the bottom oven for several hours or even overnight. Remove from the oven and allow to cool before wrapping and storing or filling with cream.

Serves 6.
....

FILLING

¹/₂ pint/300ml double or whipping cream
8 oz/ 225g fresh fruit eg raspberries, strawberries, kiwi fruit or
passion fruit

In winter I sometimes fold 2 tablespoons of chopped stem ginger and 1 tablespoon of ginger syrup into the cream. Alternatively frozen fruit selections can be stirred into the cream, but drain off the juices first. Whip the cream to a soft peak. Gently fold in half the prepared fruit. Pile this into the middle of the meringue and decorate with the remaining fruit and a few mint leaves if liked.

RICE PUDDING

....

I always think that the Rayburn would be the ideal cooker for rice pudding, cooked slowly, but I can honestly say that this is the dish that has caused me most problems with my Rayburn; and judging by the talk at my Rayburn days, other people share these problems. I know, from testing, that the use of semi-skimmed milk will not work. So no low-fat rice puddings – the more cream, the better! If you have a little cream left over, stir it in with the milk for a creamier pudding. Timing will be an estimate because all the ovens vary and we all like our puddings cooked to a different degree of thickness.

1 pint/600ml full fat milk
1 oz/25g round-grain pudding rice
1 oz/25g sugar

Put the rice and sugar in a buttered ovenproof dish. Pour in the milk. Have the oven shelf on the bottom set of runners of the top oven set at "Simmer" (130C/250F). Put the pudding in the oven and cook until a skin starts to form, about 15 minutes – this makes a creamier pudding. Continue to cook for 2 to 3 hours until a thick and creamy pudding is made.

Serves 4.

....

BREAD AND BUTTER PUDDING

....

This is an old-fashioned pudding that is popular again. Cooked gently in a bain-marie in a low oven, the custard will be just set and smooth. Before starting check that your dish will fit in the roasting tin.

3 bread rolls or brioche slices
1 oz/25g butter
¹/₄ oz sultanas (soaked in water for ¹/₂ hour and then drained)
8 fl oz/225ml milk
1 vanilla pod
8 fl oz/225ml Greek-style yoghurt
4 eggs
3 oz/75g caster sugar
a little icing sugar
pinch of salt

Cut rolls into thin slices and spread with butter. Arrange in a buttered dish and sprinkle with sultanas. Bring the milk, salt and vanilla pod to the boil.

Gently stir in the yoghurt and mix well. Mix the eggs and caster sugar together. Add the milk and yoghurt and mix well. Strain. Pour over the bread.

Stand the dish in the roasting tin. Pour hot water round the dish to about half way up the side of the dish. Slide the roasting tin into the top oven set at "Simmer" (150C/300F) towards the top for the first 15 minutes and then on the bottom set of runners for 45 minutes to 1 hour or until set.

Sieve over a little icing sugar and serve warm.

Serves 6-8.
....

APPLE AND ALMOND CRUMBLE

....

This is a slightly unusual crumble, the Amaretti biscuits provide an almond flavour with a slightly different texture. Eating apples have been used, which means that no extra sugar is needed and they cook until soft but still holding their shape.

6 crisp eating apples
juice of 1 lemon
2 oz/50g Amaretti biscuits, about 8
4 oz/100g plain flour
1 oz/25g soft brown sugar
1/2 level tsp ground cinnamon
3 oz/75g softened butter

Peel, quarter, core and thickly slice the apples. Toss in the lemon juice. Tip into an ovenproof dish.

Roughly crumble the Amaretti. Mix with the flour, sugar and cinnamon. Rub in the butter until crumbly and just beginning to hold together. Spoon over the apples.

Bake with the oven shelf on the bottom set of runners of the top oven set at "Bake" (180/250F) for about 45 minutes until the apples are soft and the top is golden brown. Should the top be browning too much before the apple is cooked slide in the cold shelf two runners above the dish.

Serves 4.
....

MAGIC LEMON PUDDING

I have been making this pudding for years, it is so popular. Now my children make it they never cease to wonder how the sauce starts on the top and ends up at the bottom!

SPONGE
4 oz/100g self-raising flour
4 oz/100g butter
4 oz/100g caster sugar
2 eggs
grated rind of 1 lemon
1-2 tbsp milk

SAUCE
4 oz/100g caster sugar
2 tbsp cornflour
juice of 1 lemon made up to $^1/_2$ pint/300ml with boiling water

Grease a 2 pint oven-proof dish. Combine the flour, softened butter, sugar, eggs and lemon rind in a mixing bowl. Beat together with an electric beater or wooden spoon until smooth and fluffy. Add milk to make a soft, dropping consistency if needed. Spread into prepared dish. For the sauce, combine the sugar and cornflour. Gradually blend in the lemon juice and boiling water mixture. Pour onto the sponge mixture. Set the top oven to "Bake" (180C/350F) and put the oven shelf on the second set of runners from the bottom. Put in the pudding and bake for 30-40 minutes. When baked, the pudding should be golden and firm on the top. The sauce will now be at the bottom. Serve hot with yoghurt or cream.

Serves 4.

VARIATION

MAGIC CHOCOLATE PUDDING
Replace the lemon rind with 1 tablespoon cocoa powder in the sponge mixture and replace the lemon juice with 1 tablespoon cocoa powder, again made up to $^1/_2$ pint/300ml with the boiling water, for the sauce.

QUICK CLAFOUTIS

....

This is a standby pudding using store-cupboard ingredients. Other types of canned fruit can be used – apricots give a more tangy taste.

14 ¹/₂ oz/410g can peach slices
1 level tbsp self-raising flour
2 eggs – beaten
15 oz/425g can or carton custard
1 tsp caster sugar

Butter a shallow oven-proof dish and dust with the caster sugar. Drain the peaches, pat dry with kitchen paper, arrange in the prepared dish. Beat the flour and eggs together, whisk in the custard. Pour over the peaches and level the surface.

Put the oven shelf on the third set of runners from the top of the top oven set at "Bake" (190C/375F), put in the Clafoutis and bake for 30 minutes until risen and golden brown. Dust with caster sugar and serve immediately.

Serves 4.
....

CHRISTMAS PUDDING

....

This is sugar-free Christmas Pudding, not that anyone except the cook would know! There is so much fruit in a Christmas pudding that no extra sugar is needed. However, it does mean that this recipe does not have the keeping quality of a sugar-rich pudding. Keep in the fridge for 2 weeks or freeze. I use plastic basins with lids, so there is no danger of the fruit attacking the aluminium dish during storage. This recipe makes one large pudding.

2 oz/50g currants
3 oz/75g raisins
3 oz/75g sultanas
2 oz/50g candied peel – chopped
2 oz/50g stoned dates – chopped
5 fl oz/150ml Guinness
1 oz/25g almonds – shredded
1 small cooking apple – grated
1 medium carrot – grated
1¹/₂ oz/35g fresh breadcrumbs
2 oz/50g vegetable suet or margarine – melted
¹/₂ tsp baking powder
pinch salt
¹/₄ tsp nutmeg – freshly grated
¹/₂ tsp ground cinnamon
1 egg – beaten
4 tbsp brandy

Grease a 1¹/₂-2 pint/900-1200ml pudding basin.

Put the currants, raisins, sultanas, peel, dates, and Guinness into a bowl, cover and leave to stand somewhere cool for 24 hours. Add the almonds, cooking apple and carrot. Stir well. Add the breadcrumbs, suet or margarine, baking powder, spices, salt, egg and brandy. Stir really well – let the whole family have a stir and a wish.

Put the mixture into the greased pudding basin. Press down and smooth the top. Cover with a circle of greaseproof paper and put on the lid or foil.

Have a pan large enough to take the pudding standing on a trivet, an old saucer or a wad of newspaper. Put the pudding in, half fill the pan with water and bring to boiling point. Simmer for 30 minutes on the simmering end of the hot plate. Put the shelf on the bottom set of runners in the top oven, set at "Simmer" (120C/240F). Put in the steaming pan and pudding for 8-12 hours or overnight. Remove from the pan and cool. Cover with fresh greaseproof paper and foil, if using, before storing.

On Christmas Day the top oven will probably be full so steam for 2-3 hours on the simmering end of the hot plate or, if your Rayburn has a cast iron bottom oven, steam the pudding for half an hour on the hot plate and then transfer to the bottom oven. Allow to stand at room temperature for half an hour before turning out onto a warmed plate. Serve with cream.

Makes I large pudding.

FRUIT FLAN – FRENCH STYLE

Do you admire the pretty French flans both in our supermarkets and in France? They are not difficult to make and are much tastier when freshly baked! Supermarkets are now selling excellent fresh or frozen pastry.

8 oz/225g rich shortcrust pastry

FILLING
2 egg yolks
2¹/₂ oz/60g caster sugar
³/₄ /20gflour good
¹/₄ pint/150ml milk
few drops vanilla essence
mixed fruits eg strawberries, kiwi, peaches, pineapples
3-4 tbsp apricot or strawberry conserve – sieved and warm

Roll out the pastry to fit a 13 x 4 x 1 inch/34 x 11cm flan tin or a 9 inch/23cm round flan tin. Chill.

To make the filling, cream the egg yolks and sugar until light and fluffy. Mix in the flour and milk. Cook over a gentle heat, stirring until thickened. Stir in vanilla essence and cool.

Bake the pastry case. Prick the base well. Set the oven to "Bake" (190C/375F). Put the pastry case on the floor of the hot top oven for 8-10 minutes until crisp and golden brown. Cool.

Remove the pastry case from the tin and stand on a plate. Fill with crème pâtissèrie.

Decorate with sliced fruits and glaze with the conserve.

Makes I large flan.

FUDGE NUT TRANCHE

An ideal winter pudding for nut lovers, this flan is made in a tranche tin. It is easy to slice, making it particularly useful for the buffet table.

PASTRY
4 oz/100g butter
6 oz/175g plain flour
1 oz/25g caster sugar
2-3 tbsp water

FILLING
4 oz/100g butter
4 oz/100g skinned hazelnuts
4 oz/100g pecan nuts
3 oz/75g soft brown sugar
5 fl oz/150ml double cream
rind and juice of 1 lemon
1 egg – beaten
6 oz/175g mixed whole nuts eg brazils, walnuts etc
2 tbsp warm apricot jam

Rub butter into flour and stir in the sugar. Bind together with the water. Roll dough to line 14 x 4 inch/34 x 11cm tranche tin.

Set the oven to "Bake" (190C/375F). Toast the hazelnuts and pecans until lightly browned on a baking tray towards the top the the pre-heated top oven. Cool and chop roughly.

Cream the butter and sugar, stir in chopped nuts, the finely grated rind of 1 lemon, 2 tablespoons of the lemon juice and the beaten egg. Beat in the cream. Pour into the flan case and arrange whole nuts on top.

Bake on the floor of the top oven set at "Bake" (190C/375F) for 45 minutes until set. Brush flan evenly with warm apricot jam.

Serves 6-8.

LEMON AND WALNUT TART

The lemon in this recipe complements the richness of the walnuts. Serve with cream or a citrus sauce.

1 sweet pastry case – 9 inch/23cm round or oblong
4 oz/100g butter
4 oz/100g soft brown sugar
2 level tbsp self-raising flour
3 oz/75g chopped walnuts
2 eggs – separated
rind and juice of 1 lemon

Cream butter and sugar until light and fluffy. Beat in the flour, walnuts, egg yolks, lemon rind and juice. Whisk egg whites until stiff, and fold them in. Pour into flan case and bake on the floor of the top oven set at "Bake" (190C/375F) for 45 minutes until golden and risen. Serve with cream or citrus sauce.

Serves 6-8.

CITRUS SAUCE

....

This is a tangy lemon sauce ideal for serving with a rich pudding such as Lemon and Walnut Tart (see page 111) or a steamed sponge pudding.

4 level tbsp lemon curd
juice and rind of 2 lemons
5 fl oz/150ml carton double cream or crème fraîche
1 level tsp cornflour
1-2 level tbsp icing sugar, sieved
water

Place lemon curd, grated lemon rinds, 4 tablespoons of the lemon juice and 4 tablespoons of water in a small saucepan. Dissolve over gentle heat.

Stir in the cream, bring to the boil and bubble for 2-3 minutes, stirring.

Blend cornflour with 2 teaspoons of cold water, whisk into the sauce, and simmer for 2-3 minutes until slightly thickened. Stir in icing sugar to taste.

Serves 6-8.

....

GERMAN APPLE CAKE

I make this when I have a glut of apples in the autumn. This cake is lovely served with thick cream for a pudding.

BASE
4 oz/100g self-raising flour
2 oz/50g soft brown sugar
2 oz/50g ground almonds
3 oz/75g butter
1 small egg or ¹/₂ standard egg, beaten
1 tsp lemon juice

FILLING
1 lb/450g cooking apples
2 oz/50g soft brown sugar
1 tsp lemon juice

TOPPING
2 oz/50g self raising flour
2 oz/50g soft brown sugar
1 tsp ground cinnamon
2 oz/50g butter

Grease and base-line an 8 inch/20cm cake tin. Sieve the flour into a bowl, stir in the sugar and 1 oz/25g ground almonds. Rub in the butter until the mixture is like breadcrumbs. Bind the mixture with the egg and lemon juice. Press into the prepared tin and sprinkle over the remaining 1 oz/25g ground almonds – this will help to absorb the apple juices. Peel and finely slice the apples and toss them in the lemon juice and sugar. Arrange the slices on the base. Sieve together the flour and cinnamon of the topping mixture. Stir in the sugar and rub in the butter. Sprinkle over the apples.

Set the top oven temperature to "Bake" (200C/400F). Put the oven shelf on the bottom set of runners of the top oven and bake the apple cake for 30 minutes. Then slide in the cold shelf to allow the cake to cook through without browning too much. Bake for a further 30-40 minutes. After this time the apples should be cooked when prodded with a knife. Cool in the tin. Dust with icing sugar before serving warm or cold.

Cuts into 8 slices.

CHOCOLATE POTS

....

These little puddings have a surprise in store. They have a solid top and are creamy underneath. They cook beautifully in a low oven. Make them well in advance to allow time to chill.

³/₄ pint/450ml milk
finely grated rind of 1 orange
6 oz/175g plain chocolate
4 egg yolks
1 oz/25g caster sugar

Pour the milk into a saucepan, add the orange rind. Heat gently on the simmering plate until boiling. Remove from the heat and leave to stand for fifteen minutes. This allows the orange flavour to infuse the milk.

Break the chocolate into a basin and stand on top of the Rayburn to melt. Beat in the egg yolks and sugar. Slowly stir in the milk. Blend well.

Strain the mixture into a jug and then pour into 6 ramekin dishes.

Stand the dishes in the roasting tin. Pour round hot water to come halfway up the ramekin dishes. Set the top oven temperature to "Simmer" (150C/300F) then slide the roasting tin into the middle of the top oven. Cook for 45 minutes or until set firm.

Remove from the roasting tin, cool and then chill.

Serves 6.
....

APPLE STRUDEL

....

Homemade strudels are easy to make now that filo pastry is so readily available. This recipe makes one large strudel, but small individual strudels can easily be made.

1 packet filo pastry
2¹/₂ oz/65g fresh breadcrumbs
2¹/₄ lb/1kg apples
4 oz/100g soft brown sugar
2¹/₂ oz/65g sultanas – optional
2¹/₂ oz/65g chopped nuts– optional
1 tsp ground cinnamon
3 oz/75g butter – melted
2-3 tsp icing sugar

Unroll the filo pastry and brush each sheet with melted butter. Lay out, layer upon layer, to make a large oblong to fit your largest baking tray or the cold shelf.

Sprinkle the breadcrumbs over the pastry.

Peel, core and thinly slice the apples. Mix together with the sugar, sultanas and nuts (if using) and cinnamon. Spoon onto the pastry sheet leaving a good 6 inch/15cm border all round. Fold in the short ends and carefully roll the strudel up so that the join is at the bottom.

Brush with any remaining butter. Set the top oven to "Bake" (190C/375F). Put the oven shelf on the third set of runners from the top and slide in the prepared strudel. Bake for 25-30 minutes until brown and crisp and the apples are cooked. Sprinkle over the icing sugar and return to the second set of runners from the top of the hot oven for 5 minutes until golden brown and glazed.

makes 8-10.

....

HOME BAKING

C A K E S   A N D   B I S C U I T S

R I C H   F R U I T   C A K E

Rich fruit cakes baked in the Rayburn are wonderfully moist and evenly cooked. Cakes cooked at simmering temperature can be left overnight and there is no need to line the cake tin. Two cakes can be baked at a time, one for you and one to give away! Cooking times vary depending on the size of the tin, the quantity of the mixture and the oven heat. However, I find that any cake put in at bedtime and removed first thing in the morning will be evenly cooked and not overdone. If your simmering oven is low on heat give the cake up to 24 hours! This recipe makes enough mixture for a 9 inch/23cm round tin or an 8 inch/20cm square tin. You can halve the recipe easily for a 7 inch/8cm round or a 6 inch/15cm square tin, or double the recipe for a 12 inch/30cm round or 11 inch/28cm square tin. This is useful for a tiered wedding cake.

1 lb/450g plain flour
¹/₂ level tsp salt
1 level tsp ground cinnamon
1 level tsp ground mixed spice
1 lb/450g sultanas – cleaned
12 oz/350g currants – cleaned
12 oz/350g raisins – cleaned
8 oz/225g glacé cherries
2 oz/50g walnuts – chopped
10 oz/300g butter – softened
10 oz/300g soft brown sugar
5 eggs
2 tbsp black treacle
finely grated rind of 1 lemon
4 tbsp brandy

Grease and line with greaseproof paper the tin needed. Sieve the flour, salt, cinnamon and mixed spice together. Stand the treacle and a tablespoon on the Rayburn to warm.

Weigh and pick over the dried fruits. Cut the cherries in half, wash in warm

water and dry. Add to the other fruit. Chop the walnuts, add to fruit.

Crack the eggs into a basin and beat well together. Grate the lemon rind.

Place the butter and sugar in a bowl and beat well until light and fluffy. Beat in the eggs, adding a little flour with each addition to prevent curdling. When all the eggs are beaten in stir in the prepared dried fruits. Fold in the flour, the lemon rind and finally the treacle and brandy. Spoon into the prepared tin and level top. Bake. Place the oven shelf on the bottom set of runners in the top oven, set at "Simmer" (150C/300F), put the cake in and bake for 8-12 hours.

To test when the cake is done, insert a warm skewer into the middle of the cake. If it is cooked, it will come out clean. Cool in the tin. When cold, wrap the cake in foil and store in a cool place.

S I M N E L   C A K E

A traditional Easter or mid-Lent Sunday cake. The marzipan in the middle leaves the cake moist and moreish.

8 oz/225g plain flour
1 level tsp baking powder
1¹/₂ level tsp mixed spice
3 eggs
6 oz/175g butter
6 oz/175g caster or soft brown sugar
8 oz/225g sultanas
6 oz/175g currants
2 oz/50g cut mixed peel
2 oz/50g glacé cherries, halved and washed
3 tbsp milk
12 oz/350g marzipan
4-6 oz/100-175g icing sugar
1 tbsp apricot jam
Easter decorations eg sugar eggs, small chickens etc

Grease and line an 8 inch/20cm round, deep cake tin. Roll out 4 oz/100g marzipan to a circle the size of the tin. Sieve together the flour, spice and baking

powder. Beat the eggs together.

Cream together the butter and sugar. Beat in the eggs, a little at a time, with 1 tablespoon flour. Fold in the remaining flour and stir in the fruit. Add milk if necessary, but do not have the mixture too soft.

Place half the mixture in the cake tin. Level the top and place the marzipan circle over it. Spread the remaining cake mixture on top and level it. Bake.

BAKING THE SIMNEL CAKE

This cake is best baked slowly in a low oven at an even temperature. It is often easiest to do this long slow cooking overnight. Set the oven to "Simmer" (150C/300F), put the oven shelf on the bottom set of runners, slide in the cake and bake for 10-12 hours or overnight, until the cake is an even, golden colour and slightly shrunk from the sides of the tin. You can test with a skewer, but the marzipan may leave a sticky mark, causing confusion. Cool in the tin.

DECORATING THE SIMNEL CAKE

Remove the greaseproof paper. Brush the top of the cake with the warmed apricot jam.

Divide the marzipan into eleven even-sized pieces. Roll into balls and place around the outside edge of the cake. Flatten tops and press on the cake firmly so that the balls are touching. Make up a thick glacé icing with the icing sugar and boiled water. Pour into the centre of the marzipan decoration.

When the icing is dry decorate with the eggs, chicks or flowers. Tie a yellow ribbon around the cake.

CHERRY CAKE

I like to make this cake in a loaf tin and serve in slices to show off the glossy cherries. Do not be tempted to mix the cherries in with a food processor or mixer, they will be chopped and won't look so attractive. If necessary fold in with a spatula at the end of mixing before putting in the tin.

8 oz/225g plain flour
1¹/₂ tsp baking powder
.¹/₄ tsp cream of tartar
pinch salt
4 oz/100g glacé cherries
6 oz/175g butter
6 oz/175g caster sugar
3 eggs
1 tbsp/15ml milk
¹/₂ tsp vanilla essence

Grease and base-line an 8 inch/20 cm round tin or a 2 lb/1kg loaf tin. Cream the butter and sugar until light and fluffy. Beat in the eggs one at a time. Fold in the remaining ingredients. Spread the mixture evenly in the tin. Set the top oven to "Bake (180C/350F) and put the oven shelf on the third set of runners from the bottom. Put in the cake and bake for 1 hour. If the cake is not cooked through, put the oven shelf on the bottom set of runners and slide the cold shelf in two runners above the top of the cake tin. The cake is baked when it has shrunk from the sides of the tin and a skewer inserted in the middle comes out cleanly.

Cool in tin for 30 minutes before turning out.

JACKY'S SULTANA AND CHERRY CAKE

This is quite a rich fruit cake, and the moist fruit gives it bags of flavour. The recipe came from my friend Jacky, and has become a firm favourite, especially with the men!

1 lb/450g sultanas
12 oz/350g glacé cherries
8 oz/225g plain flour
pinch salt
6 oz/175g butter – softened
grated rind ¹/₂ lemon
6 oz/175g caster sugar
4 eggs

Grease and line an 8 inch/20cm deep cake tin. Set the oven to "Bake" (170C/325F) and put the shelf on the second set of runners from the bottom. Cut the cherries in half and wash and dry them. Mix with the sultanas and two tablespoons of the flour.

Soften the butter with the lemon rind and cream with the caster sugar until light and fluffy. Whisk the eggs and gradually beat into the butter mixture, adding a little flour with each addition of egg. Stir in the remaining flour and the prepared fruit. Put the mixture in the cake tin and level the surface.

Put the cake into the prepared oven and bake for 1 hour. Either turn the oven down to 160C/325F or slide in the cold shelf for the next half to one hour. When cooked, the cake should be risen, golden and a skewer inserted in the middle will come out clean. Cool in the tin.

SWISS ROLL

This is my quick standby cake. It is very quick to prepare, the filling of jam is rolled in when hot. If you have only eaten shop-bought Swiss Roll you have a surprise in store, because this will be light and moist. For a summer special unroll the cake when cold and fill with whipped cream and chopped strawberries.

3 oz/75g caster sugar
3 eggs
3 oz/75g self-raising flour
3 tbsp raspberry jam
a little extra caster sugar

Grease and line a 12 inch x 9 inch (30cm x 22cm) Swiss roll tin. Sieve the flour onto a plate. Place the eggs and sugar in a bowl and whisk using an electric whisk until thick and foamy, thick enough to leave a trail.

Sieve in the flour and fold it into the mixture using a tablespoon using a cut and fold motion. Take care not to knock out the air and to keep a light, fluffy mixture. Pour the mixture into the Swiss Roll tin. Allow to level off in the tin. Set the top oven to "Bake" (200C/400F) and place the shelf on the bottom set of runners. Put in the Swiss roll and bake for 8-10 minutes until evenly brown and springy to the touch.

While the cake is in the oven put the jam to warm on top of the oven – this makes spreading easier. Lay a sheet of greaseproof paper – slightly larger than the cake tin – on the work surface and sprinkle with caster sugar.

When baked, remove the cake from the oven and immediately tip out onto the sugared greaseproof paper. Peel off the lining paper – carefully. Spread the jam evenly over the cake – take care, this is a very light cake! Starting with the shortest end nearest you roll the cake fairly tightly into a roll. Allow to cool and set with the jam at the bottom.

CHOCOLATE SWISS ROLL
Use: 2 oz/50g self-raising flour and 1 oz/25g cocoa powder – sieved.
together and used as flour.

Continue as before, omitting the jam stage. Roll up the sugared paper and the Swiss roll and allow the cake to set and cool. When cold, unroll it carefully and fill with either buttercream or whipped cream. Reroll and dust with icing or caster sugar.

CHOCOLATE SWIRLY TRAYBAKE

....

Traybakes are so useful when cooking for a crowd, or to give to coffee mornings, fêtes and so on. This recipe gives the basic quantities needed for the roasting tin. For a range of flavourings that can be used, see the variations at the end of the recipe.

4 eggs
8 oz/225g caster sugar
8 oz/225g soft margarine
10 oz/275g self-raising flour
4 tbsp boiling water and 2 tbsp cocoa powder – blended together

Line the roasting tin with foil. The easiest way is to turn the tin upside down and mould a sheet of foil over. Remove the foil gently, invert the tin and carefully put the shaped foil into the tin. Grease lightly.

Put the eggs, sugar, margarine and flour into a bowl and beat them to make a light, even mixture.

Using up about half the mixture, put spoonfuls of mixture in the prepared tin.

Add the cocoa paste to the remaining cake mixture and beat gently to blend. Fill in the spaces in the cake tin with chocolate mixture. Even the top and give one swirl to the cake with a knife.

To bake, set the top oven to "Bake" (180C/350F) and slide the tin onto the second set of runners from the bottom. Bake for 25-35 minutes until risen, evenly golden and slightly shrunk from the sides of the tin. Remove from the tin and cool. Dust with icing sugar or ice with chocolate fudge icing.

CHOCOLATE FUDGE ICING

3 oz/75g margarine
3 oz/75g cocoa – sieved
1¹/₂ lb/700g icing sugar – sieved
about 4 tbsp milk

Melt the margarine in a saucepan, add cocoa and stir over a gentle heat for 1

minute. Remove from heat. Stir in icing sugar and as much milk as needed to make a smooth, spreading consistency.

Pour over the cake, spread evenly. Allow to set before cutting the cake into squares.

VARIATIONS:
* *using the basic cake mix without the cocoa.*
* *fruit: 8 oz/225g dried fruit*
* *cherry: 6 oz/175g chopped glacé cherries*

VICTORIA SANDWICH

Sponge cakes baked in the Rayburn are spongy and moist. Do not let anyone tell you a cake cannot be made in a Rayburn – try this simple all-in-one method. I have given ideas for variations on flavours – you may want to try your own ideas. For puddings, try topping cooked fruit or jam with the sponge mixture and baking in the same way. Small cakes can be made with the same mixture – fill lined bun tins and bake for 15-20 minutes. Ice the tops to make cup cakes or fairy cakes.

3 eggs
6 oz/175g self-raising flour
6 oz/175g caster sugar
6 oz/175g soft margarine
raspberry jam to sandwich
caster sugar for top

Grease and base-line two 8 inch/20cm Victoria sandwich tins. Measure the eggs, flour, sugar and butter into a bowl and beat with a wooden spoon or an electric mixer until light and fluffy – do not overbeat. Divide the mixture between the tins and level the top. Have the oven set at "Bake" (180C/350F) and the oven shelf on the bottom set of runners. Put the mixture in the tins and bake for 25-30 minutes until golden brown and springy to the touch. Turn out onto a cooling rack. When cool, sandwich together with jam and dust the top with caster sugar.

VARIATIONS

LEMON: add the grated rind of 1 lemon to the cake mixture. Sandwich together

with lemon curd and cream. Dust with sugar.

CHOCOLATE: mix 1 tablespoon of cocoa powder with 2 tablespoons of hot water and 1 teaspoon of treacle. Add to cake mix. Sandwich together with 4 oz/100g Greek-style yoghurt and 4 oz/100g melted chocolate beaten together. Sprinkle the top with grated chocolate.

COFFEE AND WALNUT: mix 2 teaspoons of instant coffee granules with 1 tablespoon of hot water. Add to cake mix with 2 oz/50g finely chopped walnuts. Sandwich together with coffee butter icing – 8 oz/225g sieved icing sugar, 4 oz/100g soft margarine and 2 teaspoons of the coffee mixed with 1 tablespoon of hot water, beaten well together. Spread the remaining icing on top and decorate with walnut halves.

PASSION CAKE

I am not sure why this bears the name "Passion Cake", maybe because it is moist and luscious and we become passionate for the cake – or the cook! This is a truly tasty carrot cake, the best I have ever tried.

10 oz/275g plain flour
1 level tsp salt
1 level tsp bicarbonate of soda
2 level tsp baking powder
6 oz/175g soft brown sugar
3 eggs
2 ripe bananas
6 oz/175g grated carrots
2 oz/50g finely chopped walnuts
6 fl oz/175g light corn oil

FROSTING
3 oz/75g butter
3 oz/75g cream cheese
6 oz/175g icing sugar
¹/₂ tsp vanilla essence
walnuts to decorate

Sift flour, salt, bicarbonate of soda and baking powder into a mixing bowl. Add the sugar and chopped nuts. Crack in the eggs, add mashed bananas and grated carrot. Add the corn oil and beat the mixture well to make a soft cake batter.

Divide between two greased and lined 8 inch sandwich tins. Have the oven set at

"Bake" (180C/350F) and put the shelf on the bottom set of runners. Bake the cake for 30-40 minutes until risen and firm to the touch. Turn onto a cooling rack and cool.

FROSTING

Beat the butter and cheese together until soft. Beat in the sieved icing sugar and vanilla essence to make a soft and creamy frosting. Use about one third of the frosting to sandwich the cakes together. Spread the remainder on the top. Decorate with either whole nuts or chopped walnuts.

BOSTON CREAM PIE

This is a slight variation on a Victoria Sandwich that I remember my Mother making for special occasions. The cream filling is also useful for filling fruit tarts and meringues.

6 oz/175g butter
6 oz/175g caster sugar
4 eggs
8 oz/225g self-raising flour

CREAM FILLING
2 egg yolks
2¹/₂ oz/65g caster sugar
a few drops of vanilla essence
³/₄ oz/20g flour
good ¹/₄ pint/150ml milk

CHOCOLATE ICING
1 oz/25g plain chocolate
2 oz/50g sieved icing sugar
1¹/₂ tbsp water

Grease and base-line two sandwich cake tins. Cream the butter and sugar, beat in the eggs and fold in the flour. Add 1 tablespoon of warm water if needed, to make a soft dropping consistency. Divide between tins.

Set the top oven to "Bake" (180C/350F) and put the shelf on the bottom set of runners. Put in the cake tins and bake for 25-35 minutes until risen, golden and slightly shrunk from the sides of the tin. Turn onto a cooling rack and cool.

For the filling: cream the egg yolks and sugar until light and fluffy. Mix in the

flour and milk. Cook over gentle heat – stirring until thickened. Stir in the vanilla essence. Set aside to cool.

Melt the chocolate – stand in a basin on the Rayburn. Stir into icing sugar with the water. Beat well until smooth. Sandwich the cakes with the filling and pour over the chocolate icing. Leave until the icing is set.

RICH STICKY GINGERBREAD

A delicious sticky, moist gingerbread. It is good to eat on the day of making, but even nicer a day or two later. Serve in an airtight tin.

1 lb/450g plain flour
3 level tsp ground ginger
3 level tsp ground cinnamon
12 oz/355g butter
12 oz/350g soft brown sugar
6 oz/175g golden syrup
6 oz/175g black treacle
³/₄ pint/450ml milk
3 level tsp bicarbonate of soda
3 eggs

Line the roasting tin with foil and lightly grease. Sieve together the flour and spices. Stand the milk in a measuring jug on top of the Rayburn to warm.

Melt the sugar, syrup, treacle and butter in a large saucepan. Stir well over a gentle heat. Remove from the heat and stir in the flour and spices. Add the bicarbonate of soda to the warm milk. Stir the milk into the syrup mixture and beat well with a wooden spoon. Beat the eggs together in a basin. Stir into the gingerbread mixture.

Pour into the prepared tin. Set the oven to "Bake" (180C/350F). Slide the gingerbread tin onto the second set of runners from the bottom of the top oven. Bake for 40-50 minutes until risen, firm to the touch and slightly shrunk from the sides of the tin. Cool in the tin.

Cut into 20 portions.

CHOCOLATE ECLAIRS

Eclairs are actually very easy to make and fairly quick too. To make profiteroles for a pudding make the éclairs into rounds using a spoon.

CHOUX PASTRY
2¹/₂ oz/65g plain flour
pinch salt
¹/₄ pint/150ml water
2 oz/50g butter – cubed
2 eggs – well beaten

¹/₂ pint/300ml double cream, for the filling

CHOCOLATE GLACE ICING
3 oz/75g plain chocolate
1 oz/25g butter
3 tbsp warm water
¹/₂ tsp vanilla essence
6 oz/175g icing sugar

Sieve the flour and salt. Put water and butter into a saucepan, stand on the simmering plate and heat to melt the butter. Then bring to a brisk boil. Remove from the heat, quickly tip in all the flour and beat well with a wooden spoon. Return to the heat and stir briskly until the dough forms a ball and the sides of the pan are left clean. Remove from heat.

Add the eggs gradually, beating between each addition. I find a hand-held electric mixer best. Beat until a smooth, shiny mixture is formed.

Fit a piping bag with a ¹/₂ inch/1cm plain nozzle and fill it with the pastry. Pipe lengths 4 inches/10cm long on to a greased baking tray. This makes about 1 dozen.

Set the oven to "Roast" (220C/425) and put the shelf on the third set of runners from the top. Slide in the baking tray and bake for 20-25 minutes until risen and golden brown. Remove from the oven and slit the sides to allow steam to escape. Return to the oven for 5 minutes to dry out. Cool on a wire rack.

Whip cream, fill the éclairs. Cover the tops with the icing and leave to set.

CHOCOLATE GLACE ICING

Break chocolate into a basin, add the butter and stand the basin on top of the Rayburn to melt. When melted, add the water and vanilla essence. Gradually add the icing sugar, beating until smooth. Coat the éclairs. For a pudding, fill the éclairs with cream, pile high on a dish and pour the chocolate icing over them.

VARIATION: COFFEE GLACE ICING

8 oz/225g icing sugar
2 tbsp hot water
2 tsp instant coffee granules

Mix the coffee granules and hot water until dissolved. Sieve the sugar in a bowl, gradually add the coffee and beat well until the icing is thick enough to coat the back of a wooden spoon.

SHORTBREAD

This is a traditional Scottish shortbread, but I have suggested some variations to ring the changes. This shortbread, packed in a pretty box or basket makes a lovely gift. Always use butter for flavour and a crisp texture.

6 oz/175g plain flour
4 oz/100g butter
2 oz/50g caster sugar

Cut the butter into small cubes and add to the flour. Rub in well, then add the sugar. Continue to rub and work until the mixture forms a ball. Divide the mixture in two. Roll to $^1/_4$ inch/5mm thickness and 8 inch/20cm circles. Slide each circle onto a baking tray. Set the oven temperature to "Bake" (160C/350) and bake the shortbreads towards the bottom of the oven. Bake for 15-20 minutes until dry and very pale golden colour. Cool on a wire rack. Dust with caster sugar.

VARIATIONS

• Replace 1 oz/25g flour with 1 oz/25g ground rice for a slight crunch
• Use wholemeal flour
• Add 1 oz/25g finely chopped cherries
• Replace 1 oz/25g flour with 1 oz/25g ground almonds

ETHEL'S SHORTCAKE BISCUITS

....

Ethel was a dear friend of my mother's. She was a cook/housekeeper who produced delicate, tasty food. We always had these crisp biscuits with fine Earl Grey tea, but they are equally nice with fruit salads – or just straight from the biscuit tin!

4 oz/100g self raising flour
2¼ oz/65g butter
1½ oz/35g icing sugar
yolk of 1 egg

Rub the butter into the flour to the consistency of fine breadcrumbs. Stir in the icing sugar. Add the egg yolk and work it in until the dough binds together. Wrap and chill for ½ hour. Roll to ⅓ inch/1cm thickness and stamp out circles, space out on 2 baking trays. Set the oven to "Bake" (160C/350F) and bake the biscuits towards the lower half of the oven. Bake for 12-15 minutes until pale golden brown. Lift onto a cooling rack to cool and become crisp.

CHRISTMAS BUTTER BISCUITS

....

I make batches of these and give them as little offerings when visiting friends at Christmas. My children cut out Christmas shapes to give to teachers and elderly neighbours. They are truly crisp and delicious.

8 oz/225g butter
7 oz/200g caster sugar
2 eggs – beaten
1 tbsp ground almonds
14 oz/400g plain flour
1¹/₂ tsp baking powder
¹/₂ tsp salt
grated rind of 1 lemon

Cream the butter and the sugar. Add the eggs and all remaining ingredients. Knead lightly. The dough will be slightly sticky. Wrap in cling film and chill for at least one hour. Cut into quarters. Work with one quarter while the remaining three quarters stay chilled. Roll to the thickness of a 10p piece. Cut out shapes. Place on lightly greased baking trays.

Set the oven to "Bake" (160C/350F). Place the baking trays towards the lower part of the top oven and bake the biscuits until slightly golden at the edges. Cool on a wire rack. These biscuits can be iced with water icing. When baking a large batch of biscuits, remove the cold plain shelf periodically and allow to cool.

M I N C E   P I E S

My good friend Jane, who helps me with my Rayburn Cookery Days, is an excellent cook. She makes the best mince pies I have ever tasted; this is her recipe.

12 oz/350g plain white flour
8 oz/225g butter
4 oz/100g caster sugar
1 lb/450g jar mincemeat
caster sugar to dust

Sieve the flour into a bowl and stir in the sugar. Rub in the butter until it resembles breadcrumbs. Continue to rub in until the shortbread binds together. If the mixture is soft and sticky, wrap and chill for half an hour.

Roll out and cut 12 circles – not too thinly – to line the bun tins. Reroll the shortbread and cut out 12 tops. Stars and bells are good, festive shapes. Line the tins, spoon in 1 dessert spoonful of mincemeat – do not overfill. Top with the shaped lids. Set the oven to "Bake" (200C/400F) and cook the mince pies on the floor of the top oven for 15-20 minutes. Remove from the oven and dust immediately with caster sugar (it will stick on better when the mince pies are hot). This quantity will make 1 dozen pies.

G I N G E R B R E A D   S H A P E S

This makes a firm biscuit suitable for gingerbread men and other shapes, stars for Christmas, rabbits for Easter etc. Children love rolling and cutting these and when cooked they can be decorated with icing and dragees.

2 tbsp golden syrup
1 tbsp black treacle
2¹/₂ oz/65g soft brown sugar
1 tbsp water
3¹/₂ oz/90g margarine
1 level tsp ground cinnamon

1 level tsp ground ginger
pinch ground nutmeg
grated rind ¹/₂ an orange
¹/₂ level tsp bicarbonate of soda
about 8 oz/225g plain flour

Warm the syrup and treacle on top of the Rayburn before measuring. Put syrup, treacle, sugar, spices, water, margarine and orange rind into a saucepan. Bring to the boil on the simmering plate, stirring all the time.

Remove from heat and stir in bicarbonate of soda. Gradually stir in flour, beating well between each addition and making sure there are no lumps. Add as much flour as is needed to make a stiff dough. Chill the mixture, wrapped, for at least 30 minutes. The dough will now be firm enough to roll out. Roll on a floured worktop until the thickness of two 20p pieces. Stamp out shapes and place them on greased baking trays. Continue rolling and stamping out to use up all the dough. Remember to put holes in the shapes if the finished biscuits are to be hung up. Set the top oven to "Bake" (180C/375F) and bake the shapes towards the lower part of the oven until dry looking for about 10 minutes. Allow to set on the baking tray for a minute or two before removing to a wire rack.

DEMERARA CRUNCH BISCUITS

These are quick to make. The Demerara sugar gives them a crunchy texture.

10 oz/275g self-raising flour
8 oz/225g soft margarine
5 oz/150g demerara sugar
2 tsp ground ginger

Mix all the ingredients together to give a stiffish dough. Roll small walnut sized pieces into balls, and space them well apart on greased baking trays. Using a fork dipped in water, press each biscuit down gently. Set the oven temperature to "Bake (170C/375F) and bake the biscuits in the lower part of the top oven for 10-12 minutes until they are a light golden colour. Cool on a wire rack.

CHOCOLATE CHIP COOKIES

This is the best recipe for a crunchy biscuit with chunks of chocolate. Make giant cookies, one or two to a tray, for parties as going-home presents or just to fill the biscuit tin.

8 oz/225g soft margarine
6 oz/175g soft brown sugar
4 oz/100g caster sugar
1 tsp vanilla essence
2 eggs – beaten
11 oz/300g self-raising flour
8 oz/225g chocolate chips

Cream the margarine and sugars together. Beat in the eggs and vanilla essence, fold in the flour and chocolate chips. Place spoonfuls on the greased baking trays, allowing room to spread.

Set the oven to "Bake" (180C/375F) and bake the biscuits towards the lower part of the top oven for 10-15 minutes until lightly browned. Allow to set slightly on the baking tray before removing to a cooling rack.

CINNAMON BUTTER COOKIES

These are unusual chunky biscuits, ideal on their own or with fruit salad.

4 oz/100g butter
2 oz/50g caster sugar
3 oz/75g plain flour
2 oz/50g semolina
1 tbsp ground cinnamon
1 oz/25g dessicated coconut

Cream butter and sugar until light and fluffy. Sieve together the flour, cinnamon and semolina. Work dry ingredients into a creamed mixture, with the coconut. Knead lightly to give a manageable dough.

Place dough in the centre of a greased baking tray. Pat out to a 7 inch/18cm square. Neaten edges, prick with a fork. Set the oven to "Bake" (170C/375F) and put the shelf on the second set of runners from the bottom. Slide in the prepared baking tray and bake for 25-30 minutes until pale golden and looking dry. Cut into portions and cool on a wire rack.

SCONES

....

A lot of people tell me they cannot make scones. There are rules to follow: have the dough moist, a cross between a cake mix and pastry; do not take a rolling pin to scone dough; press lightly with your hand to just the thickness of your hand; bake in a hot oven.

8 oz/225g self-raising flour
1 oz/25g butter
pinch salt
$^1/_4$ – $^1/_2$ pint/150-300ml milk
one flavouring ingredient

FLAVOURINGS:
1 oz/25g sugar
2 oz/50g grated cheese
$^1/_2$ oz/15g sultanas

Sieve flour and salt. Rub in the butter. Stir in $^1/_4$ pint/150ml milk, using a knife, to make a soft but not sticky dough. Use extra milk if needed. Add the flavouring of your choice. Turn the dough onto a floured worktop – treat LIGHTLY!

Press down with the palm of the hand until the thickness of the hand. Stamp out shapes with a cutter. Place on a baking tray and brush the tops with a little milk. Pre-heat the oven to "Roast" (230C/450F) and put the oven shelf on the third set of runners from the top. Bake the scones for 10-15 minutes until well risen, golden brown and firm to the touch. Serve warm with butter. Cool to serve with jam and cream.

AMERICAN MUFFINS

....

This is a truly American recipe. Another quick cake for hungry hordes! Vary the flavourings according to what is in the store cupboard. They are good for breakfast made with wholemeal flour and served with butter and honey. Use traditional deep muffin tins or smaller English bun tins. I have used tea-cup measures – accuracy is not important.

$1^1/_2$ *cups plain flour*
$^1/_2$ *cup sugar*
$^1/_2$ *tsp salt*
2 tsp baking powder
1 egg
$^1/_2$ *cup milk*
$^1/_4$ *cup vegetable oil*
one flavouring ingredient

FLAVOURINGS:
1 cup chopped apple $^1/_2$ *tsp cinnamon*
1 oz/25g chocolate chips
$^1/_4$ *cup raisins*
$^1/_2$ *carton blueberry yoghurt*

Sieve together the flour, sugar, salt and baking powder. Stir in the flavouring of your choice. Beat the egg, add milk and oil. Stir into dry ingredients until evenly moistened.

Fill muffin tins lined with cases. Have the oven pre-heated to "Roast" (220C/425F) and the oven shelf on the third set of runners from the top. Bake for 15-20 minutes until risen and browned. Serve warm with butter.

Makes approximately six muffins.

....

MERINGUES

....

This is the best way I know to use up egg whites. This method gives a very dry, crisp meringue that can be stored for several weeks, very useful if preparing for a party. When cold, store in an airtight tin or wrap in a clean tea towel, in a basket in the airing cupboard. This is a good, dry storage place provided you do not hang damp clothes to dry in there! Because these are crisp meringues they can be filled in advance and will not go too soft.

2 egg whites
4 oz/100g caster sugar
$^1/_2$ tsp cornflour
$^1/_2$ tsp white wine vinegar
$^1/_4$ pint/150ml double cream for the filling – whipped to soft peaks

In a clean, grease-free bowl whisk egg whites until white and fluffy. Add the sugar, 1 teaspoonful at a time, whisk well after each addition.

Blend the cornflour and vinegar together, whisk in after all the sugar. The meringue mixture should be thick and fluffy.

Line a baking tray with baking parchment – not greaseproof paper. Using a dessert spoon, spoon out individual meringues onto the prepared tray.

Set the oven on a low "Simmer" (100C/200F) or "Idling". Put the meringues in the top oven and leave for several hours or overnight. If you are worried about browning, leave the oven door slightly ajar all night. This will give crisp, white meringues.

Sandwich with whipped cream up to one hour before serving.

VARIATION:
use 2 oz/50g caster sugar and 2 oz/50g soft brown sugar instead of all caster sugar for a caramel flavour

SCOTCH PANCAKES

....

These are every Rayburn-owner's standby. They are quick and easy to make when there are hungry mouths to feed and nothing in the cake tin. Guests, who always lean against the Rayburn rail, can often be persuaded to cook a batch of pancakes whilst you get on with the table-laying! Children love to make their own pancakes, especially in the shape of their initials. These can be sweet or savoury. I like them plain with crispy bacon!

4 oz/100g self-raising flour
pinch salt
1 egg
¹/₄ pint/150ml milk

Measure the flour and salt into a bowl. Make a well in the centre, add the egg and half the milk and beat well, then stir in the remaining milk to make a thick batter. Brush and then lightly grease the simmering or cooler end of the hot plate. Spoon the batter onto the simmering plate, spacing well apart, about 6 or 7 at a time.

When bubbles rise to the surface, turn the pancakes over using a fish slice. Cook for about a minute on the second side until golden brown. Lift off and keep warm on a plate in the lower warming oven whilst all the batter is being used up. Serve warm with butter. If you are making a large batch it may be necessary to put the lid down for a few minutes to warm up the simmering plate.

OPTIONAL FLAVOURINGS
1 oz/25g caster sugar
grated rind of ¹/₂ a lemon
1 oz/25g sultanas
2 oz/50g wholemeal flour and 2 oz/50g white flour
2 oz/50g buckwheat flour and 2 oz/50g white flour

WELSH CAKES

....

These are quick and easy to make and taste delicious straight from the simmering plate with lashings of real butter!

2 oz/50g butter
2 oz/50g lard
8 oz/225g self raising flour
2 oz/50g caster sugar
$^1/_2$ tsp grated nutmeg
3 oz/75g currants
1 egg
milk to mix

Rub the fats into the flour, stir in the sugar, spice and currants. Make a soft but manageable dough with the beaten egg – and milk if needed. Divide the dough in half. Pat out on a floured worktop into two rounds approximately the thickness of the hand. Cut into 8 triangles per round.

Brush the surface of the cooler end of the hot plate and oil lightly. Cook the Welsh cakes spread out on the plate, 4-5 minutes on each side to cook through. They may darken but they are still delicious. If they cook too fast on the outside or if you know the simmering plate is very hot – leave the lid up for a few minutes before starting to cook.

Serve warm, straight from the hot plate, split and buttered.

Makes 16.
....

YEAST COOKERY

QUICK BREAD

If you want to make bread, but are short on time, use this method. It is even quicker with a large capacity food processor.

1¹/₂ lb/675g strong white flour and/or wholemeal
2 tsp salt
1 sachet easy blend yeast
1 tbsp cooking oil
³/₄ pint/450ml warm water

Measure flour, salt and yeast into a mixing bowl. Stir. Add oil. Add the warm water – it must not be hot. Add ¹/₂ pint/300ml to start with and mix in to make a pliable dough. Add more water as necessary. Transfer to a floured worktop and knead for 5 minutes until smooth and stretchy.

Shape the dough into rolls or loaves. This quantity will make two small loaves or about 16 rolls. Place in well greased tins. Cover with a clean cloth. Stand on a cloth on the top of the Rayburn until doubled in size. Glaze with beaten egg. Bake in a hot oven set at "Roast" (230C/450F) – loaves on the bottom set of runners for 30 minutes, rolls on the third set of runners for 15-20 minutes.

To test if cooked, tap the bottom, if the bread sounds hollow it is baked. Cool on a wire rack.

FARMER'S BREAD

This recipe makes a moist, chewy loaf, rather different to the traditional English bread. It is delicious with cheese and pickles or slices of ham. This recipe makes 1 large loaf.

14 oz/400g plain strong white flour
5 oz/150g wholemeal flour
5 oz/150g rye flour
1 tbsp salt
1 oz/25g fresh yeast or 1 sachet easy blend yeast
8 fl oz/225ml warm water
7 fl oz/200ml buttermilk or plain yoghurt

Mix together the flours and the salt. Crumble in the fresh yeast or sprinkle in the easy blend yeast. Add the warm water and the buttermilk or yoghurt. Knead well by hand or with the dough blade in a processor to form a fairly firm dough which leaves the bowl clean.

Stand the bowl on top of a folded tea-towel on the top of the Rayburn, cover the bowl with a tea-towel and allow to rise until doubled in size, about half an hour. Knock back the dough and form into a ball. Drape the tea-towel into a bowl or basket and flour it well. Put in the dough and put to rise again until doubled in size, about 30 minutes.

Invert the loaf carefully onto a greased and floured baking sheet. Make a lattice of cuts onto the loaf's surface. Pre-heat the oven to "Roast" (230C/450F), slide the tray into the middle of the top oven. Bake for 35-45 minutes until golden, crusty and sounding hollow on the bottom when tapped. Cool on a wire rack.

PLAITED MILK LOAF

This is a rich bread that looks attractive on the bread board. It goes particularly well with home-made jam and good butter. Plaiting is not difficult and the bread rises after shaping to give a very attractive appearance.

1¹/₂ lb/675g strong, white flour
2 tsp salt 1 oz/25g fresh yeast or 1 sachet easy blend yeast
3 oz/75g soft butter
about 15 fl oz/450ml milk
1 egg, beaten, to glaze

Measure the milk into a jug and stand on the Rayburn top to warm. Measure the flour, salt and sachet yeast (if using) into a bowl. Rub in the butter.

If using fresh yeast blend this with half the warm milk. Add to the flour mixture, mixing in more milk, if needed, to make a smooth and springy dough which comes cleanly from the bowl. Knead well on a floured surface for 10 minutes, or 5 minutes in a food processor, until the dough is stretchy.

Put the dough to rise in a bowl, stand on a folded tea-towel on top of the Rayburn. Cover with a clean cloth until doubled in size, about 30 minutes. Alternatively cover with cling film (loosely) and put in the fridge overnight.

Knock back the dough and cut in half. Roll out 2 long sausage shapes. Place on a floured surface, putting one shape over the other to form an even cross. Cross over the bottom sausage of dough – retaining the cross appearance. Continue using alternate sides. When complete put the dough on its side – you will see a plait shape – and tuck in the loose ends.

Lay onto a well greased and floured baking sheet and leave to rise on top of the Rayburn for about 15 minutes until risen and puffy.

Brush well with beaten egg. Have the oven pre-heated to "Roast" (230C/450F). Put the tray of bread in the middle of the oven and bake for about 40-45 minutes until golden brown and sounding hollow when tapped on the bottom. Cool on a wire rack.

FOCCACIA

An increasingly popular Italian flat bread, foccacia is delicious with summer salads and good for mopping up excess French dressing. My recipe uses fresh rosemary, which has a strong flavour, so leave out the rosemary if you want a plainer bread.

1 lb/450g strong white flour
1 tsp salt

1 oz/25g fresh yeast or 1 sachet easy-blend yeast
4 tbsp good olive oil
about 8 fl oz/225 ml warm water
olive oil
coarse sea salt
fresh rosemary leaves

Mix the flour and the salt in a bowl. Add the dried yeast to the flour or blend the fresh yeast with a little warm water. Stir in the olive oil and most of the water, adding more water if necessary to make a manageable dough. Turn onto a floured worktop and knead for about 5 minutes until smooth and pliable. Return to the mixing bowl and cover with a tea towel. Stand on a folded tea towel on top of the Rayburn. Leave to rise until doubled in size – about 30 minutes.

Knock back the dough, roll out to an oblong about $^3/_4$ inch/2cm thick and about 12 inch x 8 inch/30 x 20cm in size. Place on a well greased and floured baking tray. Return to the top of the Rayburn to rise. Using the end of a wooden spoon handle, make deep indentations over the surface of the dough. Drizzle over about 2 tablespoons of olive oil, scatter with sea salt and the rosemary leaves.

Bake in the top oven pre-heated to "Roast" (230C/450F) with the shelf on the third set of runners from the top for about 20-30 minutes until risen and golden brown. Cool on a wire rack.

FLAVOURED BREADS

The range of breads available today can be mind boggling. I love to see what is new in the shops, but I do draw breath at the cost of some of the more exotic or interesting breads. They are easy to make, cost a fraction of the commercial variety and very often taste better. I like to make a mixed variety of breads, sometimes loaves or sometimes a ring of rolls taken from the variety made. Grease a 9 inch/23cm round cake tin, shape 8 rolls, place 7 round the outside of the tin and one in the middle. Rise and bake in the usual way. This quantity will make 2x1lb loaves. The quantity of flavourings given is enough for one loaf.

1$^1/_2$ lb/675g strong white flour
1 tbsp salt
2 tbsp olive oil

1 oz/25g fresh yeast or 1 sachet easy blend yeast
about 12 fl oz/350ml warm water
1 egg, to glaze

Put the flour, salt and oil in a large bowl. Add the easy blend yeast, or blend fresh yeast with half the water. Add to the flour mixture. Stir well, adding more water to make a smooth pliable dough. If making by hand, transfer to a floured worktop and knead for 5-10 minutes until smooth and pliable. If using a machine, 4-5 minutes kneading is sufficient. Cover with a cloth, stand on top of a folded tea-towel placed on top of the Rayburn. Leave to rise until doubled in size — about 30 minutes.

On a floured worktop divide the dough in half, knead in the chosen flavourings for each loaf. Grease and flour two 1lb/450g loaf tins or large baking trays. Shape the loaves and put them in the tins. Put to rise again on top of the Rayburn until doubled in size — again about 30 minutes. If liked, brush tops with beaten egg. To bake, have the oven pre-heated to "Roast" (230C/450F) and bake the bread in the middle of the top oven for 30 minutes. Remove from the tins — or turn upside down if using a baking sheet — return to the oven for 10 minutes until the bread is crisp and sounds hollow when knocked. Cool on wire rack.

FLAVOURINGS
One of these is sufficient for 1 small loaf:

3 oz/75g stoned olives
4 tbsp freshly chopped mixed herbs
2 tbsp chopped sun-dried tomatoes (the olive oil in the recipe can be
replaced with the tomato oil)
3 oz/75g freshly grated Gruyère or Sbrinz
3 oz/75g finely chopped walnuts

GARLIC BREAD

....

1 French stick
4-6 oz/100-175g butter, softened – depending upon the size of loaf
2-3 cloves garlic

Mash the butter in a bowl until softened. Beat in the peeled and crushed cloves of garlic. Cut the French stick into slices about 1½ inch/4cm wide – but do not cut right through.

Spread a little butter over the top. Wrap the loaf in foil and heat through in the top oven at whichever temperature it is set. Depending on the heat it will take 10-25 minutes. It is ready when piping hot and the butter has melted.

OTHER BUTTER FLAVOURS:
2 tbsp of chopped mixed herbs
2 tbsp chopped parsley
2 cloves of garlic and 1 tbsp mixed chopped herbs
3 tbsp lemon juice

BATH BUNS

Bath is my adopted city and the most attractive place to live. One traditional food that visitors to Bath always enjoy is a Bath Bun. Split and serve with good butter when freshly made.

1½ lb/675g strong white flour
1 oz/25g fresh yeast
½ tsp salt
1 tsp sugar
8 fl oz/225ml warm milk
3 oz/75g butter – melted
4 eggs
4 oz/100g caster sugar
½ oz/15g cut mixed peel
2 oz/50g currants

....

beaten egg to glaze
2 tbsp milk and 1 tbsp sugar boiled together for a sticky glaze
2 tbsp granulated sugar

Blend the yeast and 1 teaspoon of the sugar together until runny. Mix in 2 tablespoons of the warm milk. Leave for a few minutes on the Rayburn until frothy. Measure the flour, sugar and salt into a mixing bowl. In a well in the middle add the beaten eggs, the melted butter and the yeast mixture with the rest of the milk. Mix all together to make a soft, manageable dough. Do this by hand, with a mixer and dough hook or in a large processor. Put the dough on a floured work surface and knead until smooth, adding more flour if the dough should be sticky.

Return to a clean bowl, cover with a tea-towel and stand on a trivet or folded tea-towel on top of the Rayburn. Leave until the dough has doubled in size. Remove from the bowl onto a floured work surface, knock back and work in the mixed peel and the currants. Cut the dough in half, shape into 2 rounds and cut each round into 8 even pieces. Shape each piece into a bun and place on a greased baking tray. Return the tray to the top of the Rayburn on a cloth or trivet and allow to rise until doubled in size.

Brush with the beaten egg. Pre-heat the oven to "Roast" (220C/425F) and bake the buns in the top oven for 15-20 minutes, until risen, golden brown and sounding hollow when tapped. Immediately on removing from the oven brush with the sticky glaze and sprinkle over the granulated sugar. Cool.

Makes 16.

JAMS AND PRESERVES

STRAWBERRY JAM

....

This method of making strawberry jam is quick and easy. It also gives a fresh bright colour and taste.

7 lb/3kg strawberries
juice of 2 lemons
6 lb/2.5kg sugar

Hull the strawberries and discard any soft or mouldy fruit. Put in a large non-metallic bowl with the lemon juice. Add the sugar, stir gently, cover and leave to stand overnight.

The next day, transfer to a preserving pan and heat on the cooler end of the hot plate to dissolve the sugar. Stir gently to avoid breaking the fruit. Slide to the boiling end and boil rapidly for 10-15 minutes until a teaspoonful of the mixture wrinkles after setting for 1 minute on a cool saucer. Cool the jam for a few minutes – this prevents the fruit floating to the top of the jar – before putting into warmed jam jars. Cover and seal in the usual way.

Makes about 10 lb/5kg.
....

RASPBERRY PRESERVE

Raspberries are probably my favourite fruit. Eating them today brings back memories of picking pounds of them on summer evenings. My father grew enough for us to eat and to make into a wonderful fresh-tasting jam. This method of preserving raspberries keeps their fresh flavour and is lovely in the depths of winter with fresh scones for tea. This recipe does not make a firm-set jam, but a soft, bright preserve.

4 lb/1.8kg raspberries
5 lb/2.25kg sugar

Rinse and pick over the raspberries. Spread out in a large roasting tin. Measure the sugar and spread out in a second roasting tin or two smaller tins. Place the sugar and raspberries in the top oven set at "Bake" (200C/400F) and heat for 30-40 minutes, occasionally stirring. Heat until the raspberries are soft and can be broken down. The sugar should be hot.

Remove from the oven and combine the sugar and raspberries. Stir well until the sugar has dissolved. Ladle into warm jars. Cover and label in the usual way.

Makes about 8 lb/3.5kg.

GOOSEBERRY JAM

....

This is a lovely sweet, tangy jam. It is very easy to make because it sets so easily. Ripe, red dessert gooseberries will give quite a pink jam, the more usual green gooseberries will give a more yellow jam.

4 lb/1.8kg gooseberries – topped, tailed and washed
1 pint/600ml water
4 lb/1.8kg granulated sugar
small knob of butter

Put the gooseberries and the water in a large preserving pan. Place on the simmering end of the hot plate and bring slowly to the boil. Simmer until the fruit is cooked. Stir in the sugar and the butter. Stir well until the sugar has dissolved. Move to the boiling plate, bring to the boil and boil vigorously for 10 minutes. Remove from the heat and test for set. Pour into clean, warm jars and finish in the usual way.

Makes about 8 lb/3.5kg.
....

KIWI PRESERVE

....

When my stocks of jam are running low and there is little fruit about, I make this jam as kiwis are often on offer in supermarkets.

1¹/₂ lb/750g Kiwi fruit
¹/₂ pint/250ml water
2 tbsp lemon juice
1 lb/500g granulated sugar

Peel and finely chop the Kiwi fruit. Place in a heavy based pan with the water and lemon juice. Bring to the boil, cover and move to the simmering end of the hot plate until the fruit is softened, 20-30 minutes. Remove the lid and reduce the mixture to a pulp. Add the sugar and stir until dissolved. Bring to the boil and boil rapidly without stirring for about 15 minutes. Watch carefully, you need a good boil, but it must not boil over. Remove from the heat, and test for a set, when a teaspoon of the mixture wrinkles after setting for 1 minute on a cool saucer. Remove any scum and pour into warmed, sterilised jars. Cover with a wax disc, cool, and then cover with a lid and label.

Makes 2 lb/1 kg.
....

MARMALADE

....

Homemade marmalade has a tang that commercial marmalade never matches. Even if you do not eat much yourself it always makes welcome gifts and contributions to charity stalls. Seville oranges are available in January and February, so I find that if I am too busy at that time of year I freeze some oranges until I have some time. I do not find extra pectin is needed as mentioned in some books. This recipe is for a Seville orange marmalade, but the same method and quantities can be used for lemons and grapefruit, just make up to 3 lb/1.35kg fruit. For a dark marmalade add 1 oz/25g dark treacle with the sugar.

3 lb/1.5kg Seville oranges
juice of 2 lemons
4 pints/2.5 litres water
6 lb/2.5kg sugar

Scrub the oranges and put in a preserving pan. Add the lemon juice and water. If the oranges bob to the top, put in an old plate to keep them below the water level. Bring to the boil, cover and either allow to simmer for 2 hours on the hot plate or to reduce heat loss and steam in the kitchen, in the top oven set on "Simmer" (150C/300F) for 4-5 hours.

Remove the pan from the oven. Scoop out the oranges and allow them to cool enough to handle. Cut in half, scoop out the flesh and the pips and return them to the liquid. Bring the orange liquid to the boil and boil with the lid off for 5 minutes. Strain through a sieve squeezing out all the juices.

Cut up the orange peel as fine or coarse as you like. Put half the prepared peel into the preserving pan along with half the strained liquid and 3 lb/1.25kg sugar. Place on the simmering plate and stir until all the sugar is dissolved.

Move to the hotter end of the hot plate and boil rapidly for 10-15 minutes and test for a setting point. When this point is reached allow the marmalade to sit for 10 minutes so that the peel will not rise to the top in the jars. Pour into warm, sterilised jars, seal and label as for jam. Repeat with the remaining ingredients.

Makes about 10 lb/4.5kg.
....

INDIAN CHUTNEY

....

This recipe has been a firm favourite in our family for many years. I am not sure of the origin. It gives a rich, sweet chutney, lovely with cheese and cold meats.

1 lb/450g apples – peeled, cored and chopped
1 lb/450g onions – peeled and chopped
1 lb/450g ripe tomatoes
1 lb/450g raisins
1 lb/450g sultanas
1 lb/450g brown sugar
1 tsp ground ginger
1 tsp cayenne pepper
1¹/₂ tsp fresh curry powder
2 oz/50g salt
³/₄ pint/450ml malt vinegar

Mix the spices with some of the vinegar. Put all the ingredients in a large pan, stand on the simmering plate and heat, stirring, until the sugar is dissolved and the mixture is boiling. Either slide along the hot plate to the cooler part and simmer the mixture until soft, about 1 hour, or transfer to the simmering oven set at "Simmer" (150C/300F) for 1-1¹/₂ hours. On the hot plate, boil slowly until the mixture is thick and brown. Pour into warm, sterilised jars.

Makes about 6 lb/2.75kg.
....

LEMON AND LIME CHUTNEY

A chutney to serve with curries, it is best to make this when lemons or limes are on special offer in the shops. It needs to mature for at least a month after making, but it gets better with keeping

4 lb/1.8kg lemons or limes – or mixed
2 lb/900g onions
2 oz/50g salt
¹/₂ oz/12g cardamom pods
¹/₂ oz/12g coriander seeds
2 pints/1.2 litres white wine vinegar
2 oz/50g green chillis – chopped
4 oz/100g fresh ginger – grated
3 lb/1.35kg sugar

Slice the fruit and remove the pips. Put into a large bowl with the salt and the finely sliced onions. Tie the spices together in a muslin bag and add to the bowl along with the vinegar. Cover and leave to stand for 8 hours or overnight. Pour the mixture into a heavy-based preserving pan, add the chilli and ginger. Bring to the boil on the simmering end of the hot plate, cover and allow to simmer for 1-1¹/₂ hours, either on the hot plate or in the top oven set at "Simmer" .(150C/300F), until the fruit and onions are softened.

On the simmering plate, add the sugar, stirring constantly to dissolve the sugar. Move to the boiling spot and boil fast for 15-20 minutes. Stir frequently to prevent burning – it is a good idea to wear an oven gauntlet to protect your hand from splashes. It may be sufficient to have the pan on the cooler part of the hot plate, but still keep a good boil going. Boil to reduce the liquid and make a thickish consistency – it will thicken as it cools.

Remove the spice bag. Ladle the chutney into warm, clean, sterilised jars. Cover and seal while hot. Keep for at least one month in a cool, dark place before opening.

Makes about 8 lb/3.5kg

SUGAR-FREE MINCEMEAT

I developed this recipe for my mother when she became a diabetic and I felt she should not miss our on all festive treats. I used it with puff pastry to make mincemeat slices. With all the dried fruits in mincemeat there is no need for sugar, and to prevent fermentation I put the mixture in a low simmering oven for 4-5 hours, the mincemeat will keep for at least 12 months – if there is any left. Make enough to wrap decoratively for presents and to use some during the year. Mincemeat is a wonderful stuffing for baked apples.

1 lb/450g cooking apples, peeled, cored and coarsely grated
8 oz/225g shredded suet or vegetarian substitute
12 oz/350g raisins
12 oz/350g sultanas
12 oz/350g currants
grated rind and juice of 2 oranges
grated rind and juice of 2 lemons
2 oz/50g slivered almonds
4 tsp mixed slice
1 tsp ground cinnamon
$^1/_2$ grated nutmeg
6 tbsp brandy

Mix together all the ingredients except the brandy. Mix very thoroughly; I get the family to make this on a wet Autumn afternoon and everyone has a good stir. Cover with a plate or a cloth and leave for at least 12 hours in a cool place. Stir again. Set the oven to "Simmer" (125C/275F), put the shelf on the bottom set of runner in the top oven and put in the bowl of mincemeat, covered. Leave for 4-5 hours. Remove and set aside until cold. Stir in the brandy. Spoon into clean dry jars. Cover with wax discs, seal and label.

Makes about 5 lb/2.25kg.

INDEX